FILIPINO
STICK FIGHTING
TECHNIQUES

The Essential Techniques of
Cabales Serrada Escrima

MARK V. WILEY

With a new foreword by
Darren G. Tibon

TUTTLE Publishing

Tokyo | Rutland, Vermont | Singapore

"BOOKS TO SPAN THE EAST AND WEST"

Tuttle Publishing was founded in 1832 in the small New England town of Rutland, Vermont [USA]. Our core values remain as strong today as they were then—to publish best-in-class books which bring people together one page at a time. In 1948, we established a publishing office in Japan—and Tuttle is now a leader in publishing English-language books about the arts, languages and cultures of Asia. The world has become a much smaller place today and Asia's economic and cultural influence has grown. Yet the need for meaningful dialogue and information about this diverse region has never been greater. Over the past seven decades, Tuttle has published thousands of books on subjects ranging from martial arts and paper crafts to language learning and literature—and our talented authors, illustrators, designers and photographers have won many prestigious awards. We welcome you to explore the wealth of information available on Asia at **www.tuttlepublishing.com**.

Disclaimer: Please note that the publisher and author(s) of this instructional book are NOT RESPONSIBLE in any manner whatsoever for any injury that may result from practicing the techniques and/or following the instructions given within. Martial arts training can be dangerous—both to you and to others—if not practiced safely. If you're in doubt as to how to proceed or whether your practice is safe, consult with a trained martial arts teacher before beginning. Since the physical activities described herein may be too strenuous in nature for some readers, it is also essential that a physician be consulted prior to training.

Published by Tuttle Publishing, an imprint of Periplus Editions (HK) Ltd.

www.tuttlepublishing.com

Copyright ©2019 Mark Wiley

Library of Congress Cataloging-in-Publication in Process

ISBN: 978-0-8048-5141-1

DISTRIBUTED BY

North America, Latin America & Europe
Tuttle Publishing,
364 Innovation Drive,
North Clarendon, VT 05759-9436 U.S.A.
Tel: 1 (802) 773-8930; Fax: 1 (802) 773-6993
info@tuttlepublishing.com
www.tuttlepublishing.com

Japan
Tuttle Publishing
Yaekari Building, 3rd Floor
5-4-12 Osaki, Shinagawa-ku,
Tokyo, Japan 141-0032
Tel: (81) 3 5437-0171; Fax: (81) 3 5437-0755
sales@tuttle.co.jp
www.tuttle.co.jp

Asia Pacific
Berkeley Books Pte. Ltd.
3 Kallang Sector #04-01,
Singapore 349278
Tel: (65) 6741 2178; Fax: (65) 6741 2179
inquiries@periplus.com.sg
www.tuttlepublishing.com

24 23 22 21
9 8 7 6 5 4 3 2

Printed in Malaysia   2108VP

TUTTLE PUBLISHING® is a registered trademark of Tuttle Publishing, a division of Periplus Editions (HK) Ltd.

For Jeraldine and Alex

In memory of Grandmaster Angel Cabales.
May his legacy live on....

TABLE OF CONTENTS

LETTER OF PERMIT FOR MARK WILEY

For many years I have received prospects from people for writing a book on my style of escrima; Cabales-Serrada. I had turned down all of these offers, feeling uneasy with the idea of my art being available in picture for anyone to see. However, with the spread of my art as it is going and my inability to preserve it everywhere, I find it time to document Cabales-Serrada Escrima by means of a six volume series.

I have chosen Mark Wiley, one of my few chosen master instructors, to present my work in these books. This series will cover all aspects of escrima from the fundamentals to the advanced training and techniques. I highly recomend this and every book in Mark's collection to anybody who seeks the ultimate, complete documented knowledge of an art. Mark Wiley is, in my opinion, an honest and humble person and a true master in every sense; to promote Cabales-Serrada Escrima.

Angel Cabales
Grandmaster
Cabales-Serrada Escrima

FOREWORD

Filipino Stick Fighting Techniques: A Guide to the Essential Techniques of Cabales Serrada Escrima, is an outstanding introduction to the art of Cabales Serrada Escrima and the teachings of its founder, Grandmaster Angel Cabales. The author, Mark Wiley, outlines the basics of the art as well as the concepts behind Angel Cabales' teachings. Tradition, respect, peace and harmony, camaraderie, discipline of mind and body, being the best that you can be, and striving for excellence are essentially the values of Cabales Serrada Escrima and the book does an outstanding job of presenting them. It has been over twenty years since its original publication and Wiley's book remains an essential resource for anyone interested in escrima.

I actually first became interested in escrima when I learned of a connection to the art in my family history. My great-grandfather, Marcos Tibon, was an escrimador from Cebu, Philippines, and I grew up hearing many stories about him. I also heard about how Filipinos lived in those days from my father, Eugene Tibon, Sr., an amateur boxer who also studied Goju-ryu karate, and, in the late sixties to early seventies, serrada escrima with Grandmaster Angel Cabales.

At 7 years old, I entered the disciplined realm of martial arts. I am the youngest of five children. My siblings and I were automatically enrolled in the "Tibon's Backyard Martial Arts School," where my father began our training. At age 11, my brother, Eugene Tibon, Jr., and I were enrolled in our first Goju-ryu dojo under the same instructor my father had trained with. I continued training in Goju-ryu under my brother's tutelage until my mid-twenties.

My second private instruction of the fundamentals of the Cabales serrada system of escrima came from my cousin's husband, Joseph Reasonable, an advanced instructor under Grandmaster Cabales. He introduced me to Angel Cabales in 1981 during one of his classes on California Street located in downtown Stockton, California. Joseph and I worked together on the night shift in a steel fabrication shop where break time became instruction time. There he was able to cover the twelve basic angles of attack with me. In 1982, I met Vincent Cabales, Grandmaster Angel's son, who was hired at the same shop. Vincent and I became very good friends. It was undoubtedly evident that I was destined to pursue a life with serrada escrima.

Angel Cabales instructs Darren Tibon.

Through Vincent Cabales, I met Gabriel Ascuncion, another advanced student under Angel Cabales. Gabriel and I exchanged martial arts knowledge—Goju-ryu for serrada escrima. This training was more extensive than I previously received, and it was during that training with Gabriel that I decided serrada was the art I wanted to master some day. I finally got to join the Cabales Escrima Academy in 1987, the year my son, Chez Tibon, was born.

Although I had previously trained with two of his advanced students, Grandmaster Cabales started my training from the very beginning, and I also learned about the history of serrada through him. I eventually made my way up in the academy and

Darren Tibon with brother Gene Tibon.

received my advanced diploma and master's degree. Angel often taught privately at his house to students from out of town and out of state. I would frequently get calls from him to come over and help instruct these students. I was more than happy to help Angel in any way that I could because that is the type of relationship we had. I felt very close to him, like a grandson. I considered Grandmaster Angel Cabales, his wife, and his younger children, to be a very big part of my life. And all these years later I still do today.

In escrima, I had found what I was looking for, a martial art that was born from the island of my ancestors. Escrima is the connection that links my great-grandfather, Marcos Tibon, to me, passed down through my father's generation. Now it is ready to be passed to yet another generation—my children and my family.

After Grandmaster Cabales passed away in 1991, Jerry Preciado and I opened a school and named it Angel's Disciples Escrima Association. It was originally open to all the masters and advanced students who studied under Grandmaster Cabales to come and train freely in an effort to keep serrada alive. Understandably, some of the other masters went their own way to represent serrada as they felt best. However, we kept the school in the same place that Grandmaster Angel taught during the last years of his life, and have done so ever since. It is a sentimental place and our way of keeping fond memories alive of our late master. I will promote serrada escrima as best I can for as long as I can, and I urge and support everyone with the ability to do the same.

Teaching serrada is my way of giving back to Angel while preserving my ancestral heritage and living up to the knowledge he bestowed on me. The good will to all who are willing to teach, all who are willing to sacrifice their time and effort to further the spreading of knowledge to others, should be applauded. There are other masters of the late Grandmaster Angel Cabales out there who have an enthusiastic and positive attitude toward promoting and preserving serrada, like Mark Wiley who has written this excellent book. I feel honored to be one of so many actively preserving Grandmaster Angel's teachings.

Darren G. Tibon

Darren Tibon

INTRODUCTION

This is a revised and expanded edition of my previous effort, *Filipino Martial Arts: Cabales Serrada Escrima.* There are several reasons why I have reworked the material. First, as evidenced in the Letter of Permit, Angel Cabales, the art's late founder, initially asked me to write a series of six books on his art of serrada escrima. (His original outline for the series is presented in Appendix B). However, in that no Filipino martial art books had been published or distributed on a large scale in the United States in the ten years prior to my letter of inquiry, the publisher was unsure as to the sales potential of such a series. Therefore, the material for the proposed series was condensed into a single volume; space limitations restricting it from including training methods, advanced concepts, or fighting strategies.

Second, I was only nineteen years old when I began writing the aforementioned book (I am now thirty-one), and had not previously written anything. Since that time, though, I have done a great deal of writing—actually making it my profession—and feel that as a more seasoned writer I am now better able to present the art to the reader. I guess one could say that it was the request of my late teacher to write a book on his art that was the turning point in my life in terms of a career path.

Third, since the publication of the first edition in 1994, I have had the opportunity to travel to the Philippines a dozen times to conduct field research on escrima in general, and on Felicisimo Dizon, Angel Cabales, and the Doce Pares Society in particular. Much of this research has not heretofore been published. I have also had the privilege of meeting a number of the art's most senior practitioners, among them Dentoy Revillar, Mike Inay, Rene Latosa, and Art Miraflor. And while these individuals have all since developed their own systems, they were gracious enough to share with me their individual recollections of the early history of Cabales serrada escrima in the United States. Moreover, I invited the art's senior masters and instructors to submit essays in their own names to be included in this edition, wherein they could offer their individual perspective on Angel Cabales and his fighting art.

Fourth, given my full-time profession in publishing, my ongoing anthropological studies and research, and my wish to spend as much time with my family as possible, I am no longer an active escrima instructor. And while I still maintain my personal training several days a week, I only teach a few private pupils. What free time I do have is spent perpetuating the arts through research and writing. With this in mind, I wanted to take the photographic focus of this book off me, in an effort to promote instructors in the art who are actively teaching it. Thus, the technique photographs included herein feature a number of instructors of the art who trained with Grandmaster Cabales at different periods in time.

Fifth, while working as editor and publisher of a number of leading martial arts book and magazine companies, I have read, proofed, edited, and/or published hundreds of martial arts manuscripts. I am of the opinion (and I am not alone in this) that the old way of presenting the martial arts in terms of footwork, techniques, self-defense, and so on, in prefabricated, unimaginative, and disconnected ways, is no longer viable or useful. The martial arts reader has gone beyond such mundane presentations. But to better present an art, those elements that make it effective must be identified and duly addressed.

So what is it that makes an art effective? Is it the individual footwork, stances, strikes, blocks, counters, and disarms? Or is it the long hours spent training and sparring? The answer is: yes and no. Therefore, the sayings, "An art is only as good as its techniques," and "An art is only as good as the individual practitioner," are both narrow and limiting. Moreover, the question of what makes an art effective is perhaps the wrong question to ask. It would be more useful for the practitioner to ask the question, "How can I make this art useful for me?"

In general, an art eventually becomes "useful" to an individual—or an individual finally becomes able to effectively apply an art—only after an understanding of the interconnectedness and interrelation of each of the art's individual components to the whole has been acquired (whether tacitly or explicitly). And the most direct way of coming to this deeper understanding of an art is by identifying the underlying concepts, principles, and strategies of its individual techniques and realizing how they relate to, and indeed depend on, one another. With this in mind, the phrase "An art, its techniques, and the ability of its practitioners to apply it effectively, are only as good as its underlying concepts, principles, fighting strategies, as developed and honed through its interconnected training methods," is perhaps a more correct way of considering things.

I have therefore attempted here to present the art of Cabales serrada escrima in a conceptually-based format. To do this, I have refrained from illustrating set techniques that must be memorized against each of the system's angles of attack. Rather, I have explained the individual defensive concepts in terms of how and why they each work and under what conditions they are best utilized.

It is hoped that this method of presenting this art will allow the diligent reader to realize that regardless of a technique's expression or combination, as long as a movement does not breach the prescribed concepts, principles, and strategies of the art, it is still Cabales serrada escrima. Therefore, there is truly no need to memorize between three and fourteen single-stick counters for each of the twelve strikes—as is the standard—for an understanding of what makes one type of counter more effective against a particular type of attack. This allows the practitioner to move freely and effectively, without having to remember or to build into muscle memory a preset defensive technique for every possible attack. And since there are far too many types and combinations of possible attacks, there is simply no way to memorize counters to all of them. Thus, by extending the concept of "angle of attack" to the concept of "method of counterattack," one can learn to freely maneuver within the art and practice a single defense against many types of attacks from the onset.

With this in mind, the book is divided into six sections, each building on the previous one and presenting a different facet of the art in relation to the whole. Part One briefly outlines the contemporary history of escrima in general to the development and perpetuation of the Cabales serrada system in particular. Part Two gives the reader various "keyholes" through which to view the art, by offering personal accounts of students' training with Cabales at different points in time. Part Three lays the foundation of the physical art by discussing the fundamental body positions of the art, the concept and methods of controlling distance, the dynamics of blocking and striking, and an analysis of the system's twelve strikes. Part Four describes and illustrates the art's core single-stick defensive methods, while Part Five describes and illustrates the art's core empty-hand defensive system. Part Six illustrates drills for developing coordination, reflexes, timing, and distance, in addition to discussing the mindset necessary when facing an opponent. The book concludes with an Afterword, and two Appendices for those who seek further information. It is hoped that this new material sheds more light on Angel Cabales and the history and development of Cabales serrada escrima by offering the reader a broad perspective.

I am grateful to Tuttle Publishing for allowing me to write this revised and expanded presentation of Cabales serrada escrima, and to all who were involved in its publication. It certainly was not an individual effort. I extend my deepest gratitude to the late Antonio Ilustrisimo, Antonio Diego, Modesto Madrigal, Jose Mena, Abner Pasa, Fred Lazo, Krishna Godhania, and Abondio Baet, for sharing with me their insights into the history of escrima in general, and for relating to me their firsthand stories of their interactions with the Doce Pares Society, Felicisimo Dizon, and/or Angel Cabales in the Philippines.

To Leo Giron, Dentoy Revillar, Art Miraflor, Mike Inay, Rene Latosa, Frank Rillamas, J.C. Cabiero, Darren Tibon, Jerry Preciado, Ron Saturno, Khalid Khan, Carlito Bonjoc, Jr., Anthony Davis, Sultan Uddin (Kimball Joyce), and Alan McLuckie, for sharing with me (at various times over the past 15 years) their anecdotes and insights into Angel Cabales and his art in the United States.

To Gabriel Asuncion, Carlito Bonjoc, Jr., Vincent Cabales, Sr., Vincent Cabales, Jr., Anthony Davis, Joe Gastello, Michael Keyes, Frank Lile, Art Miraflor, Jasen Posadas, Jerry Preciado, Anthony Rillamas, Frank Rillamas, Ron Saturno, JoJo Soriben, Darren Tibon, and Stanley Wells for posing for the technique photographs illustrating the techniques presented herein.

To Tony Somera (heir apparent of Giron arnis escrima) and Joel Juanitas (Bahala Na historian), for working together with me to extinguish 30 years of bad blood between the escrima groups of Angel Cabales and Leo Giron, for helping to bring the serrada masters together for our 10-year reunion, and for taking the technique photographs for this book.

To Chuck Cadell, Khalid Khan, Art Miraflor, Jerry Preciado, Darren Tibon, Tony Somera, Alan McLuckie, Carlito Bonjoc, Jr., and Rene Latosa, for allowing me to reproduce photographs from their personal collections.

To Gilbert Johnson, Dan Inosanto, and Jane Hallander for their early writings on Angel Cabales and serrada escrima. It was their stories that inspired me to seek out this man and study his art.

And to Alexander D.C. Kask, for giving me an unbelievable window of opportunity.

Thank you all.

—Mark V. Wiley
Towson, MD

CHAPTER 1

HISTORY OF
CABALES SERRADA ESCRIMA

Centuries old, the Filipino fighting arts have long been a staple of Filipino society. They have played integral and often history-changing roles in the defense of the Philippines and survival of the Filipino. There are several hundred styles of these fighting arts presently being preserved and taught throughout the Philippines. Although known by many names—often descriptive of the styles and names of their founders and enemies—Filipino martial arts can be classified into five general categories: 1) fighting arts of the Indigenous Filipinos, 2) fighting arts of the Muslim Filipinos, 3) classical fighting arts of the Christian Filipinos, 4) contemporary fighting arts of the Christian Filipinos, and 5) modern Filipino interpretations of martial arts brought into the Philippines from other countries.

The Classical Art of Escrima

It is the classical and contemporary fighting arts of the lowland Christian Filipinos—commonly known under the generic rubrics of *escrima* and *arnis*—that are the most widely practiced in the Philippines and around the world today. These systems were traditionally steeped in *baston y daga,* or the concurrent use of a twenty-six inch stick and a twelve-inch dagger. Over the years, the single stick has come to the fore in many of these systems as their primary weapon.

The popularity of the arts of arnis and escrima began to resurface on the island of Cebu during the 1920s, at which time a number of martial arts practitioners began to openly teach their arts. In 1920, the late Venancio "Anciong" Bacon, the founder of Balintawak arnis, opened the Labangon Fencing Club—the first "commercial" arnis club in Cebu. Following Bacon's lead, Johnny Chiuten, Islao Romo, and the Cañete brothers began openly teaching their respective styles of stick-fighting. The Philippine Olympic Stadium also began to promote full-contact arnis tournaments in the 1920s.

Grandmaster Angel Cabales

The art of Cabales serrada escrima traces its lineage from Stockton, California to Sudlon, Cebu. It is a system whose core techniques and movements are reminiscent of the stick and dagger systems that originated in Cebu during the early part of the twentieth century. It is not surprising, then, that one can find undeniable similarities in the systems of Balintawak arnis, kalis Ilustrisimo, decuerdas escrima, and Cabales serrada escrima. And like its sister arts, the single stick eventually became the primary weapon of the Cabales serrada system. It is important to note that although the *serrada* method of fighting is common in the Philippines, the art of Cabales serrada escrima per se did not historically exist there. It is a system that was developed by the late Grandmaster Angel Cabales in the United States in the 1960s, stemming from his background in Western boxing, decuerdas escrima, and his own personal innovations.

Dizon and Doce Pares

It was in the 1930s that the prominent *escrimadors* in Cebu and neighboring islands came together in the interest of perpetuating their indigenous fighting arts. To do this, in 1932 they organized the Doce Pares Association, which became the driving force behind the reemergence of Filipino martial arts and their integration into Filipino society. After the six Cañete brothers joined Doce Pares in 1939, political differences led a number of original members, such as Anciong Bacon, to separate themselves from the group. It was then that Eulogio Cañete became the new Association president—and the Cañetes have headed it ever since.

Angel Cabales often told stories of how his master, Felicisimo Dizon, was not only a member of Doce Pares, but was one of its most prominent fighters. He related how at a young age Dizon wanted to study under one of the greatest exponents of escrima, a hermit who lived in a secluded cave. In order to reach the hermit, Felicisimo had to courageously climb a steep mountain cliff. Upon reaching the top, he had to dive into a shark-infested lagoon, and then swim through an underground cavern to the hermit's dwelling. This was done to prove his loyalty and dedication to the master.

Dizon was said to have learned the *decuerdas* style of escrima from this hermit. As Dizon's abilities improved, he wanted to try out other renowned *escrimadors*. In those days, the phrase "try out" literally meant a fight to the death.

Dizon was said to have never turned down a challenge, and he would fight for nothing less than the death of one or both participants. As a result of his newfound reputation as a survivor of over a dozen "death matches," Felicisimo Dizon was admitted into the Doce Pares Society, a brotherhood of the most renowned fighters of the area.

The final test of the Doce Pares Society was what some say came to be known as the "decuerdas tunnel" (so-named after Dizon's fighting style). The tunnel was void of light, and its walls were fashioned with an array of hardwood sticks and sharp steel blades. The floor was rigged with crude foot levers that were triggered by pressure. As an escrimador advanced through the tunnel, he would inevitably step on one of the levers and release one of the weapons from the wall, which would strike out at him. Before he engaged in a test of skill and fate in the tunnels, an escrimador's family would have a coffin prepared and waiting for him in the event that he was unsuccessful. Dizon, too, had his coffin prepared, as he honestly thought that he would not succeed in emerging from this tunnel alive. He did, and was said to be the only person ever to emerge from the tunnel unscathed.

To say the least, not only were many of Cabales' students surprised to hear such a fantastic story, but so, too, were the members of the Doce Pares Association, who claimed the story was false. The suspect nature of Cabales' claims concerning Dizon and Doce Pares stem from three basic facts: 1) the hermit's cave and the so-called decuerdas tunnels have yet to be located in Cebu; 2) the style of Cabales and the Cañete's appear to be diametrically opposed; and 3) the officers of the Doce Pares Association have kept detailed records of the various masters and students who came through their association, and Felicisimo Dizon's name is nowhere to be found.

When I questioned Cabales further on this issue, he said that Dizon was not with the Cañate's Doce Pares Association, but was a member of a much older Doce Pares Society that was formed somewhere in southern Luzon more than a century ago. When I questioned a number of senior Doce Pares Association members about the notion of there being an older society by the same name, they flat out rejected the idea and instead submitted that Dizon was only a minor master in Cebu, who used to sit and observe their practice, but would not join in.

It wasn't until 1994—when I made my first research trip to the Philippines—that the stories of an older Doce Pares Society again surfaced. While in Manila I met and interviewed on several occasions the late Antonio Ilustrisimo and Jose Mena, both former friends of Dizon and Cabales. While Mena was unable to elaborate on the Doce Pares Society, Ilustrisimo had some interesting information. It appears that Ilustrisimo's uncle, Agapito Ilustrisimo, became a spiritual leader on mystical Mt. Banahaw, located in Laguna province, southern Luzon, and that the original Doce Pares Society originated within the caverns of this holy mountain.

Independently of this, my *ngo cho kun* teacher, Alexander Co, gave me a locally published book by Vicente Marasigan—a teacher and writer of popular religiosity—titled, *A Banahaw Guru: Symbolic Deeds of Agapito Illustrisimo* (Ateneo de Manila, 1985). This book is a translation of an original religious document with the translator's commentary. While the story of Illustrisimo's "calling" to act as a spiritual leader begins in 1935, the book nonetheless provides some important and relevant information relating to Cabales' story.

Grandmaster Antonio Ilustisimo   **Grandmaster Jose Mena**

In answer to the question of the viability of digging and living in mountain caves, many of which were made in southern Luzon, Marasigan translates as follows: "The next day, Ama said that they would first work on the cave at Tanag. They made a Templo in Tanag, and those digging were the people from Balibago, Luntel, Palingkaro, and Lian. Ama again departed but told them to continue digging. . . The next morning, they resumed the work of digging and boring the cave. . ." (page 156: 88a). And "Afterwards, they went to Balibago and built a cave there. And when they were digging, Ama said: 'On the other side of that log, you will find two holes where you will take something.' They continued digging and they found the two holes, and in them, a skull and a small knee-cap, and these were entrusted to the care of Mr. Poruso" (page 157: 89). And further, "The next day, they returned to widen the cave" (157: 90).

In support of the claim that Dizon could have swam through a lagoon to enter the hermit's cave, it should be noted that Mt. Banahaw is located in Laguna, which was so-named because of its many large lagoons. Marasigan translates as follows: "The next cave to be dug was under the basement of the Central, and it was in that cave that the dignum wood was obtained for making canes and clubs used for exercise. These used to be made by old Costan and Candido. This cave was quite terrifying when those who worked there would come out, they would be bent and dizzy. At the bottom of the interior of this cave, there was water, said to be a sea, and witnesses testified that they could hear cockcrow inside" (158: 94a).

And in defense of a Doce Pares existing in Mt. Banahaw, Laguna, Marasigan translates as follows: "There was a meeting in the Templo; Ama summoned Octoman, Fortunado, Jesus, and Pedro. 'Remember this, my sons, you represent the Doce Pares and the apostles, and you are responsible for this place: Kinabuhayan. . . .'" (185: 157f).

After interviewing Cabales, Ilustrisimo, and Mena, the heretofore fantastic story of Felicisimo Dizon, his hermit master, the cave and tunnel, and the Doce Pares Society started to come into focus. There were only two things that I felt were needed to validate this story beyond a doubt, and they were: 1) to travel to Laguna and try to locate either members of the Doce Pares Society or associates of Felicisimo Dizon and 2) to make a trek to Mt. Banahaw to see these caves and interview the religious dwellers there firsthand. And while I have yet to visit Mt. Banahaw, I did travel to Laguna in 1999.

Grandmaster Madrigal

My trip to Laguna was organized by Abondio Baet, one of the area's leading masters. It was through Baet that I was able to meet, interview, and "play" with six of the province's leading masters: Modesto Madrigal, Reynaldo Baldemor, Rogelio Alberto, Gregorio Baet, Daniel Baet, and Abondio Baet. And while all of these men were familiar with the Doce Pares Society, it was Abondio Baet and Modesto Madrigal who were able to supply me with information on Felicisimo Dizon.

According to them, the Doce Pares Society was founded by a group of twelve escrimadors on Mt. Banahaw more than 200 years ago. Moreover, whereas the Doce Pares Association of Cebu translates their name as "twelve pairs" of hands or strikes, the Doce Pares Society of Laguna translates their name as a society of "twelve peers" of equally-skilled men.

Although a Cebuano, Dizon was eventually permitted to join the Society because of his skills in escrima and possession of highly powerful *oracion* (prayers) and *anting-anting* (amulets). According to Madrigal and Baet, an escrimador's spiritual powers was the true test of admittance into the Society. In proving their skills, some escrimadors would swing a *bolo* from their hand at a bamboo tree ten feet away, and be able to cut through it from a distance, or cut loose the fruit from its branches.

In proving his oracion and anting-anting, Dizon emerged unscathed from the "decuerdas tunnel," known in Laguna as *kuweba ng kamatayan,* or "cave of death." The only other Society member whose name can be recalled during Dizon's time is Julian Madrigal. Madrigal passed on the art to five students: Rofu Baguio, Felipe "Garimot" Baet (the father of Abondio Baet), Apolinar de Jesus, Pedro Magracia, and Modesto Madrigal. Modesto Madrigal, now 78 years old, is the last known disciple of the Doce Pares Society.

The Doce Pares Society disbanded in the 1930s, because many of the members lost interest and belief in the spiritual dimensions of the art. With the disbanding of the Society, Dizon headed for Manila, where he eventually became employed as a security guard on the Tondo shipping piers. It was while working the piers that Dizon befriended a young man named Antonio Ilustrisimo.

According to Antonio Diego (the heir of kalis Ilustrisimo) Dizon used to train together with Ilustrisimo and Antonio Mercado in San Nicholas, an area near the waterfront. The fighting arts of these men are similar because not only do they all hail from Cebu, but the men became training partners in Manila.

While many assume that Dizon, Ilustrisimo, and Cabales were contemporaries, they were not. In fact, Dizon was said to have been around 20 years older than Ilustrisimo, who himself was 13 years older than Cabales. So while they may have eventually been part of the same group, Dizon was the elder and more experienced, followed by Ilustrisimo, and then Cabales. In fact, Ilustrisimo told me of how he used to hold Dizon's sword for him when awaiting his challenger's arrival for a match. Another member of their training group was Floro Villabrille, the younger cousin of Ilustrisimo. Although both Cabales and Villabrille practiced with Dizon and Ilustrisimo, it was at different times, so they never met. As perspective, Villabrille was 4 years older than Cabales.

During the Second World War, Dizon, Ilustrisimo, and Pedic Naba joined up with the Filipino guerrillas to fight the invading Japanese forces. Toward the end of the war, Ilustrisimo tells of how the three of them were called on to round up the Filipino traitors, and execute them by cutting off their heads with *barong* (leaf-shaped swords).

Dizon, like Ilustrisimo and Cabales after him, eventually took work as a seaman, where he would not only take on challengers at other seaports, but also use his spiritual powers to heal the sick. According to Fred Lazo, a one-time student of Dizon, in his later life Dizon suffered a number of strokes that left him confined to a chair, and eventually he died of a heart attack in the early 1970s. Although he has passed on, the core of Dizon's art has been spread around the world through the efforts of his student, Angel Cabales.

Angel Cabales

Angel Cabales was born on October 4, 1917, in Barrio Igania, Sibalom, Antique, on the island of Panay. Life for Angel began with a series of bad turns. Two weeks after his baptism, his mother, Marta Oniana, passed away. Upon hearing the news of his wife's death, Melcher Cabales went crazy, sold his slaughterhouse, and moved to Mindoro Island, abandoning his three sons, Vincent, Canuto, and Angel.

Angel and his brothers were lucky because their aunt and uncle took them in and raised them as their own. Cabales' aunt was a midwife and she took on the sole responsibility of raising Angel and his brothers after her husband's subsequent sudden death. The four of them were fortunate, for they never lacked food or shelter. During the farming off-seasons, Cabales' aunt would lend what extra money she had to local rice farmers, and in turn she would receive rice from them during harvest times.

Throughout his childhood Angel dreamed of becoming a professional boxer. One day in 1932, when Angel was fifteen, he witnessed some of the *barrio's* young men fighting with sticks. Curiosity aroused, Cabales learned that they were in fact practicing the art of escrima, which was taught to them by a master named Felicisimo Dizon. After four months of pestering Dizon, Angel was finally accepted as his personal student.

Realizing that he was more suited to stick-fighting than boxing, Cabales immersed himself fully in his newfound obsession: escrima.

At age seventeen, Cabales opted for the more exciting life of the big city. Going alone, he packed his bag and traveled to Manila. The first year was tough for him as he tried to survive by working various odd jobs. Cabales had no formal academic education; he claimed his wisdom came from the streets. Then in 1937, he gained decent work experience working as a foreman for the Madrigal Cement Factory in Rizal, a province near Manila. Cabales worked there for 1 year before returning to Manila, at which time he had little trouble finding work.

To his surprise, Cabales met up with Dizon again while working the Tondo shipping piers in Manila. It was here that Cabales also befriended Antonio Ilustrisimo, in addition to others, and they would all train together at night.

After a hard day's work, the men would frequent the many local bars. In those days, girls, rice wine, and trouble came easy. It was then that Cabales fought in a number of challenge matches—some to the death. Through these experiences, Cabales, like Dizon, learned to appreciate the highly practical aspects of escrima.

Tired of violence and attracted by stories of wealth and prosperity overseas, in 1939 Cabales became a seaman aboard the cargo ship *Don Jose*. This vessel traveled to many ports around the world, including various places along the coastal United States.

As seafaring adventurers usually have it, these were not relaxing times. Long hours of labor with little money and food left an air of restlessness about the ship. Cabales and his friends often found themselves pitted against others they came across on their journeys. Many of Cabales' friends were killed as a result. Aboard the ship, Cabales became involved in an altercation that led to the coining of his slogan: "Three strikes and a man will fall." One day he was approached by a man claiming to be an escrimador and was asked if he would like to "practice." He already knew what to expect because in those days, the word "practice," like "try out," meant a fight to the finish. Without hesitation, Cabales obliged this man, and with the third motion of his stick, the man fell and was never to get up.

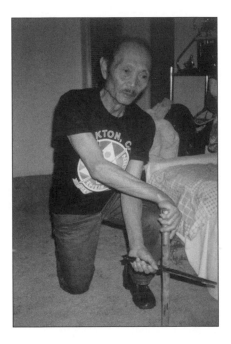

Leaving a life of danger aboard the *Don Jose,* Cabales jumped ship off the coast of California. Upon coming ashore, he found a temporary home in a small Filipino community in San Francisco, where he made some extra money teaching a few private students the rudiments of escrima.

In 1945, no doubt in search of further adventure, Angel Cabales traveled north to Alaska and found work in the canneries and fisheries. After a short stay, as the result of yet another confrontation in which he severely injured three men, Cabales moved back to California. For the next 20 years, he worked as a foreman in the Stockton asparagus fields.

Life in Stockton was no less eventful. Once again Cabales built his reputation through escrima. After his arrival, he was asked by many to openly teach his art. Angel initially turned down these requests, feeling uneasy with the idea of teaching others how to counter the very skills that had kept him alive. He did, however, begin teaching a number of students privately in his many apartments during the mid-sixties. It was during this time that individuals like Dentoy Revillar were first exposed to his art.

In 1966, Max Sarmiento, Angel's friend, student, and business partner, urged Cabales on, telling him that the future of escrima rested in his hands and that he should open a public academy. Actually, the idea for the academy was that it was to be a group effort. While Angel was to be the chief instructor, Leo Giron and Max Sarmiento would also teach their respective arts there, while Dentoy Revillar (a student of all three masters) would be available to instruct should one of the masters not be able to attend. Politics being what they are, the masters had a falling out, which led Cabales to open the academy on his own. And according to Dentoy Revillar, while many believe the academy was opened in 1966, it was actually March of 1967 that Angel Cabales opened the first public Filipino martial arts academy in the United States, thus earning him the title "Father of Escrima on the Mainland USA."

Angel Cabales instructs Max Sarmiento in escrima.

During the last 25 years of his life, Angel Cabales taught thousands of people versed in a multitude of martial styles. He gave annual demonstrations and exhibitions throughout California and much of the United States. During the 1970s, Cabales made two instructional films with his assistant Jimmy Tacosa for Koinonia Productions. He also made an appearance opposite Leo Fong in the movie *Tiger's Revenge,* where he demonstrated the art of escrima.

Angel Cabales and Jimmy Tacosa give a demonstration.

During the last three years of his life, Cabales' health began to desert him. With open-heart surgery behind him, he fought the odds, disregarded doctor's orders, and continued to teach a packed schedule of private students and biweekly classes at his academy located next to Gong Lee's restaurant on Harding Way in Stockton, California.

In September 1990, Angel Cabales was admitted to the hospital ravaged by walking pneumonia. What the doctors found, after a series of tests were run, was a cancerous tumor in his right lung. After 3 months of chemotherapy, which proved to be ineffective, cancer was also detected in his liver.

Serrada masters Jerry Preciado and Darren Tibon pose with their students.

Before he died, Grandmaster Cabales asked Darren Tibon and Jerry Preciado, two of his master graduates, to take over his academy. Feeling uneasy with the idea, since both had ties with Angel's son Vincent, they declined and instead suggested that Angel leave it to his son. Cabales then turned his academy over to his son Vincent, who, although a master of the art, had been inactive for much of the previous decade. As his health deteriorated, more and more people began to come out of the woodwork looking for rank certification, especially a number of Angel's former students, trying one last time to get what they were previously denied. It was to Cabales' credit, however, that despite his need for financial stability and the need to feed his wife and two young children, he turned down bribes for certification.

Vincent Cabales

On March 3, 1991, at 11:15 A.M., Grandmaster Angel Cabales passed away. He left this world having led the life of a warrior: true to himself and his beliefs, and never afraid to take a stand.

Grandmaster Angel Cabales had certainly done more than his share of promoting and spreading the martial arts of the Philippines. In 1991, Angel Cabales was posthumously inducted into the Black Belt Hall of Fame as "Weapons Instructor of the Year."

Angel Cabales' tombstone.

During the quarter century that Angel Cabales had publicly taught his art of escrima, thousands of people had passed through the doors of his escrima academy. It is truly amazing, in a world of exploitation and self-proclamation, that Grandmaster Cabales had never lost sight of his ideals or compromised rank for political reasons. Forty-nine years after his arrival in the United States, Cabales had only awarded sixteen of his nearly seventy instructors the rank of Master. It is the quality of his master graduates that gives credibility to his system, not the quantity.

10 years after Cabales' death, Masters, teachers, and
students gathered to support the publication of this book.

CHAPTER 2

DEVELOPMENT OF THE CABALES SERRADA SYSTEM

While many use the terms "style" and "system" interchangeably, there is indeed a difference between them.

A "style" is a personal way of expressing or performing a set of defined techniques. It is also often a synonym for a method or category of techniques within a specific art. What a style is not, however, is a system.

A "system" is an organized set of basics and techniques taught and practiced in an orderly fashion and progressing from one point to another. A system is not a bunch of loose techniques or drills thrown together and practiced on a whim. That, on the contrary, is merely unorganized and incorrect training.

In wasn't until after World War II, when a number of well-structured martial arts filtered into the Philippines from places like Japan and Korea, that there developed defined training curriculums in escrima and specific names were given to the practitioners' respective personal "styles." In the past, one merely learned and mastered what one needed to survive and picked up what one could along the way or through one's own experience-based innovation. The contemporary "structuring" of the Filipino arts was done with the idea of keeping in tandem with the way the arts of other countries were able to grow and spread around the world.

From a Style to a System

According to Angel Cabales, what he learned from Felicisimo Dizon was a cata-log of stick and dagger and single-stick fighting techniques—a "style" of fighting. Moreover, the term *decuerdas* refers to hundreds of threads intertwined until they form a length of rope. Figuratively speaking, decuerdas refers to the interconnected basics or core movements of a fighting style or system. Thus, according to Modesto Madrigal, when people said that Dizon was a master of decuerdas, they weren't referring to the name of his style. Rather, they meant he was a master of the core fighting techniques of escrima. And this is why there are so many practitioners in the Philippines who use that term to describe their art, even though they may have no direct lineage link between them.

According to Dentoy Revillar, when he first started studying under Cabales before the public academy was opened, Angel did not have a name for his art; he merely called it escrima. It wasn't until after the Cabales Escrima Academy was opened that an old Filipino man came by to observe. After class one day, the old man remarked to Angel, "Your art has many *mga serradas*," meaning it has many "closing techniques." A few weeks later, Dentoy recalls Angel coming to class and announcing that his art was now called Cabales serrada escrima.

After opening his academy, Angel taught the students just as he did when teaching them privately: he would have everybody pair off, and he would go from person to person and instruct them one-on-one. However, as the classes grew in size, there came a need to develop a more structured way of teaching groups and having students progress. Even though all of the information on each student was in his head, other practitioners and soon-to-be instructors of the art did not know how much the others had learned, and thus what to teach them when Angel was not around.

Cabales' original course of instruction in the sixties only consisted of stick-and-dagger and

Master Dentoy Revillar, head of "SLD Escrima."

single-stick training. It was after he opened his academy that some basic empty-hand techniques were introduced into the system. According to Art Miraflor (a student of that era), Angel started introducing low front kicks into the curriculum because his assistant, Dentoy Revillar, started to teach them in class. Cabales then added a knee strike and a chop behind the neck, but only after bending over an opponent with a locking technique. The empty-hand blocking and locking techniques were added one by one over the years as Angel developed them. Since he had not learned hand-to-hand techniques in the Philippines, Cabales merely translated certain stick defenses (such as the cross-block and outside block) to the empty-hands. This was because people tended to shy away from learning escrima, as they wanted to learn an empty-hand self-defense system, as opposed to a weapon art.

By the mid-seventies, Angel had developed a strong training curriculum, which included single-stick techniques, empty-hands locking, and both stick and unarmed disarming techniques. By 1975, he had put into place a definitive ranking structure, with the aid of his assistant Mike Inay, that graded students as either Basic, Advanced, or Master Instructors.

Cabales based his rankings on the core of the system: the theory and use of twelve strikes or angles of attack. Each numbered angle represented a level of achievement for the student and introduced new material. So new students would first learn the required defenses against strike one before progressing to strike two, and so on.

Another teaching method Angel used—and one that advanced the student through the core techniques of the system faster—was to teach three basic single-stick defenses against each of the twelve strikes.

Regardless of which method he used to teach, after the students learned defenses against the fourth or fifth angles, Angel would introduce them to drills for developing reflexes, coordination, distancing, and timing. Through a drill known as "lock and block" (wherein a student armed with a single stick must defend himself against an opponent aggressively attacking with a stick and dagger) and another drill known as "flow sparring" (wherein students exchange an even number of blocks and strikes in succession), the aforementioned attributes would be developed.

The first advanced degrees were awarded to Dentoy Revillar, Dan Inosanto, Richard Bustillo, and Jimmy Tacosa. Angel also stated at the meeting where he awarded these certificates, that the master's degree would "only be awarded to those who were not [only] highly skilled but also loyal to Cabales serrada escrima." From that meeting until his death in 1991, Angel Cabales only awarded 16 master's degrees.

Progressions in Training

The basics of any art are truly the building blocks of an effective combat system. Mastery of the fundamental concepts is a must in order to progress in an effective and efficient manner. All of the advanced principles and techniques are based on the premise that one has a strong foundation and working knowledge of the basics. And so it is with Cabales serrada escrima.

Early Serrada student Mike Inay with Angel Cabales. Mike is now the head of his own "Inayan Eskrima" system.

Beginners in this art are first taught how to measure their stick, which equals the length of an extended arm, from the armpit to the wrist. They are then taught how to assume the basic fighting stance, how to maneuver along an isosceles triangle, and how to execute the system's twelve strikes.

Once these basics are learned, practitioners are taught three basic single-stick defenses against the first five angles of attack. After angle five is learned, they move on to the system's core training drills, known as "lock and block" and "flow sparring." After a level of sufficient skill is achieved with the basic skills in these drills, students are taught three basic single-stick defenses against the remaining seven angles of attack.

Along the way, three basic empty-hand parries, a set of sixteen joint-locking techniques, and methods of disarming an opponent while performing the above-mentioned counters, are also taught. It is at this point that a student will graduate to the rank of basic instructor, and receive the "basic diploma."

To be awarded the system's "advanced diploma," students must learn between six and fourteen single-stick counters against each of the twelve angles of attack, be able to perform disarms during the course of each counter, be able to incorporate the new techniques into the "lock and block" drill, and use and defend against them in "flow sparring." In addition to the new defensive techniques, practitioners at this level are also taught methods of feinting, or drawing openings in an opponent's defenses—a skill known as "picking"—as well as methods of countering their opponents counters of their techniques—a skill known as "reversing."

To graduate with a "master's degree," practitioners of Cabales serrada escrima must demonstrate perfect execution of all of the preceding blocks and counters in the system, as well as be able to articulate their finer points and theories. New material introduced includes techniques in the knife, stick, and dagger; methods of maneuvering from the inside to the outside and from the outside to the inside of an opponent's attacks; methods for countering a long stick with the system's short stick; and methods of "sticky stick" and "reverse reversing." At this point, a student's training is considered complete. And it was only in the last years before his death that Angel instructed his few remaining active master disciples in the final techniques of the art, such as *reserrada* and *fraile,* which he had previously kept for himself.

Like any true art form, Cabales serrada escrima is a living entity that grew and evolved as its founder did. The progression from individual training to group instruction led to changes in teaching methods and the inclusion of empty-hand techniques to attract the public. The inclusion of a ranking structure made it necessary to divide and expand the core curriculum. And while the art originally used a 26-inch stick, it was the wish of the students to become faster than one another that led to the art embracing the shorter 24-inch stick and eventually the 18-inch stick, which is in wide use today. As a result of use of the short stick, Cabales coined the phrase: "I can block a mile-long stick with only eighteen inches."

The Path of Proficiency

Motivation is a basic component in the study of any discipline; it is what leads you toward the achievement of your individual goals. You must objectively consider what it is that motivates you toward achieving success in the martial arts. Are you motivated by of quantitative incentives (such as money) or qualitative ones (such as status)? On the other hand, you may be motivated by the fear of failure in a physical confrontation. Your mental outlook on your training, which is rooted in motivation, will determine your individual behavior, both in the training school and outside of it. When you are motivated, you become directed and focused and can therefore clarify in your mind what your individual motives are for obtaining proficiency in escrima. Once you have achieved this clarity you must set specific long- and short-term goals for yourself without expecting immediate results in areas beyond those that are realistically attainable at that time.

To become proficient in any skill takes dedication, hard work, and an unbending desire. Time and dedication to practice are the main ingredients in achieving greatness in escrima. There is simply no substitute for putting in the long hours of earnest practice. Actually, it is not so much the number of hours you put into your training, as the results that you get out of each one that counts. There are truly no shortcuts to attaining proficiency; it requires years of dedicated, quality practice time. The path of proficiency is a long and arduous one, but the fruits of your labor will be more than compensation.

Repetition is a key factor in any skill that requires a high degree of coordination. A good way to practice escrima is to repeatedly perform all the footwork, strikes, and techniques while facing a mirror. In this manner, you can see your mistakes and determine if the correct body positions and coverage are present. Another way to develop perfection in techniques is to break them down into their respective parts (e.g., wrist movement, hip rotation, breath control, torque, speed, power). By repeatedly performing each individual movement in a sequence, the sequence as a whole will greatly improve. Dedication and repetition of movement will anchor the techniques into the body and breed proficiency in their application.

I once asked Grandmaster Cabales why he never did left-handed stick-work; he always held a stick or sword in his right hand and a dagger in his left. "It is more important to be one hundred percent prepared to defend against an attack," he answered, "than to only have fifty-percent proficiency on two sides." Cabales continued, saying that an escrimador's right and left hands have their respective jobs and to train them to perform with unbeatable precision is what wins a fight; having only half-proficiency on two sides would be useless if you were up against an experienced opponent.

I understand his point of view and can attest to its effectiveness, having sparred with him many times, only to effectively land just a handful of blows in exchanges of over forty. However, death matches are highly uncommon in our modern world. When training from a combative standpoint, Cabales' theory cannot be contested; when training from a holistic and artistic perspective, ambidexterity is a must.

Tennis players and baseball pitchers often suffer from a spinal disorder that results from over-development of certain muscle groups on one side of their body. This is also the case with practitioners of escrima who do not train for ambidexterity Just as a bodybuilder lifts weights to develop evenly distributed muscle groups for a well-balanced body, so must the martial artist strive for a symmetrical body. Therefore, while developing proficiency on both your right and left sides may hamper your ability to perform in a death match, the health benefits far outweigh the chances of most of us ever engaging in one.

By training hard in the basics and following the progressions in this book, a good understanding and skill in the art of Cabales serrada escrima can be gained. To progress to a higher level, you must go beyond the written word and seek a qualified instructor. The secret to unlocking personal talent and skill is to be willing to question what it is that you are learning. By questioning, I do not necessarily mean doubting, but rather an intellectual approach to finding permutations of already existing techniques and concepts. Innovation is your best teacher, because it can teach you many things that you subconsciously knew but never physically performed. Train hard and spar with as many people of different weapon and empty-hand systems as you can. In this way, you will experience first hand how Cabales serrada escrima can work for you.

PART II:
REFLECTIONS OF THE GRANDMASTER

CHAPTER 3

IN HIS OWN WAY

I am of the philosophy that art—any art—is always greater than the individuals who try in earnest to express themselves within it. Moreover, in my attempt to not perpetuate the cult of personality so prevalent in this field, in my previous writings I have refrained from including information on myself so as to eliminate the thought that I write out of self-promotion rather than for the promotion of the art. As a result of this omission, however, many readers expressed to me that they wanted to know what it was like training with the legendary escrima master, Angel Cabales.

After further consideration, I realized that I had omitted an important part of the socialization process so necessary in the martial arts, as in life. That is, the looking to our past for heroes and masters to emulate, skills to aspire to, and stories of training and relationships to offer a sense of belonging, of being part of the inner circle of the arts—a folk group, if you will. And so, I offer just a few vignettes here with the hope of shedding light on the personality of my teacher, and how he interacted with students coming to him from out of town, as I did.

Since I did not live in Stockton, my personal training with Grandmaster Cabales was necessarily time-limited. As a result, our training sessions were long and specific. On arriving in Stockton, I would spend a few weeks at a time in his home, training in his living room or on his enclosed front patio. We would wake up early in the morning to start training from defenses against strike one, and progress from there. He would strike at me slowly, and forbid me to counter with speed. He wanted to be sure that I understood and had digested every detail of every counter, and the only way to do so, he asserted, was to do them slowly and deliberately. Cabales said that anyone can move fast, but to move fast with improper technique only leads to defeat. "Even if you are slow," he would say, "as long as your movements and timing are precise, you can defeat anyone."

Mark V. Wiley with Angel Cabales.

The next morning, we would arise and begin again from defenses against strike one. No matter who came to learn from Angel, or how long they had studied, if there was a break in training he always began them again from counter one against strike one. And this he did with me every morning during my trips, to make sure I had truly digested the information he had taught me the previous day.

Every day we trained for no less than 14 hours. We stopped only to eat or run some errands. There are two rather amusing incidents that I recall vividly regarding these errands that I would like to share.

One time Angel had given me his latest Cabales serrada tee-shirt, which was bright red with his logo on the front. Angel's wife, Teresa ("Tess"), had asked us to take his young son Gelmar and his young daughter Marygel to the store to buy some ice cream. On entering the store, I noticed a group of street toughs staring in our direction. Being the honest and naive young man that I was, I thought they were just angry at something and not necessarily looking at me. For some reason I told Angel about them and he said, "Yeah, it's the Crips." I replied that I didn't know who the Crips were, and Angel explained to me that they were the rival gang of the Bloods, and the two gangs are identified by the colors they wear. I asked him what that had to do with me, and Angel replied with a chuckle, "The Blood's color is red, and you're wearing my red shirt!" Nothing happened, and although it was nerve-wracking at the time, I laugh fondly at the memory of it now. After all, Angel must have known that the red shirt I was wearing would have attracted someone's attention; maybe he wanted to have me test my skills for real. . .

Mark V. Wiley, Kimball Joyce, Angel Cabales, Alan McLuckie

On another occasion, Angel and I took his young children to Chuck-E-Cheese, the children's theme restaurant. I fondly remember Angel playing video games with his young children and buying them pizza, especially since he was in his seventies at the time. And every time we got into his big boat of a car, in which the ceiling lining was always hanging down, Angel would say, as if it just happened, "My kids just tore down my roof. I will fix it for you right away." I would laugh to myself at this every time, because it was nice that the old warrior was concerned about the quality of his guest's stay.

While Angel mostly trained me in private, on Mondays and Wednesdays, he would take me to his academy to train with his few active senior students, including Darren Tibon, Jerry Preciado, Frank Rillamas, and Rey Tap. It was these individuals who were present when I finished my training and was awarded my master's degree from Grandmaster Cabales on March 14, 1990. It was a day I will never forget, and an honor I will never abuse.

After training each night, Angel would tell me stories of how many of his earlier students left his organization to align with the teachers in Southern California to become politically stronger, or to start their own styles. He wasn't as sad as he was angry at them, because it seemed that every time he awarded someone his advanced diploma, they would leave and open up their own competing school in town and call it a different art. He would even call his other senior students, such as Frank Rillamas, to come and talk with us in his kitchen, and they would complain about this person or that teaching serrada to another rival escrima group in Stockton, or this or that person graduating and never being heard from again. In retrospect, I get the impression that the point of the conversations was not so much to let me know who not to align myself with, as it was to let me know that I was to stay true to what Angel was passing on to me, because it was a great privilege.

In not wanting to either let Cabales down or forget what he taught me, I used to practice every movement at home by jamming a stick between the books on my shelf. It was through this method and by obsessively watching video tapes of our training sessions to memorize every detail of what he did, that I was able to progress in this art prior to opening my school and having students of my own to practice on.

One event really hit me on a gut level with regard to what this man sacrificed for me. One night as I walked out of what I thought was his guest room to use the bathroom, I nearly stepped on Angel's head. All this time, and while in his seventies, he had given up his personal bed for me and sacrificed his own health and well-being by sleeping on the cold, hard floor! From that night on, despite the fact that he refused to sleep in his bed while I was visiting, I slept on the floor right next to him.

In not wanting to single out my own reminiscences as being somehow more important than another's, the following chapters feature essays given to me by a number of Cabales' other students. Since these individuals trained and interacted with our teacher at different periods in time, it is hoped that the following chapters will offer a more well-rounded perspective on Angel Cabales and his art of serrada escrima.

CHAPTER 4

ART AND ANGEL

By Art Miraflor

My family moved to Stockton, California in 1968, when I was 16-years old. I was brought up in a very good Christian environment. As a teenager, I did not get into a lot of trouble—it's probably that I just didn't get caught. My dad, Job Bing Miraflor, asked me one day, "Do you want to learn a martial art?" I didn't know what martial art meant; I thought it was a new dish or game.

After visiting six or seven schools I became a little disappointed. At the judo school, they were grabbing and throwing students all over the mat, which, being under 100 pounds, scared me. The tae kwon do school was doing some mean kicks that looked too hard for me. The karate school was really hitting hard, grabbing, and throwing. Also not my style.

Then one day, my dad was at his doctor's office, Dr. Bernadino, who happened to be a Filipino. My dad asked him if he knew of any Filipino martial arts schools in town. He replied that the only one he knew of was open to the public. He gave my dad Grandmaster Angel Cabales' address on Harding Way and El Dorado streets, next to Gong Lee's Chinese restaurant (still good food by the way).

After being disappointed by the other schools, within 30 minutes I made up my mind this art was it. I told my dad I wanted to start right away, and said I thought I could whip everybody in the class. Of course he told me to zip it!

Art Miraflor

I came from a family of four girls and four boys, and we didn't have a lot of money, so my dad decided to sign just me up. After several months, my dad started to pay for my younger brother Abel B. Miraflor, who at thirteen became my sparring partner.

When I first met Angel Cabales, he had this big smile that would squint his eyes, he had a strong grip, and he was short in stature. I said to myself, How bad is this dude? Only later did I find out how deadly he really was.

Angel told my dad it would be twenty dollars a month and that practice was held on Monday and Wednesday nights, from 7:00–9:00 P.M. I always made sure I was the first to get to class to help my master open the doors and carry in the bag of sticks.

When we talked to some of the other schools, they said only the black belts or advanced students could practice with sticks—I guess for control. What I liked about this class was that you started off the first night with a stick in your hand.

When I started in 1968, Angel did not have any paperwork—not an application, a clipboard, a flier, charts, not even certificates. So since everything was in his head, you had to be at every class consistently, listen very well, and attempt to understand what he was trying to say over his strong accent.

Angel Cabales strikes at Dentoy Revillar.

I don't remember the names of all the students who were there when I started, but there were about five of us. I think his school had started only a year and a half earlier, so he was just getting the word around. Besides Grandmaster Angel, the next head instructor was Dentoy Revillar (whom I've always had respect for as one of the fastest escrimadors around), and the top student was Rene Latosa (this guy was fast and serious).

One of Angel's students was Kathy Lee, the daughter of the owner of the building and restaurant next door. This girl was deadly; I've seen her hit so hard she knocked the stick out of Angel's hand several times. She would come to visit wearing a minidress and high heels, always dressed up, and she would ask who wanted to practice. Most students started to hide because she was good, and they didn't want to get hit. As of this writing, she is now the Head Clerk for the City of Stockton.

I enjoyed practicing in the old studio. It had a lot of room and that old rustic look, something like what you see in the movies, and the old wood floor was the best. Angel would spar or do "lock and block" with Dentoy, and his shoes would get clacking—it sounded like he was tap dancing.

The first night I started training I had to borrow a stick from Angel. One of the first things he taught me was how to hold the stick. We used a 24-inch stick for the most part. He told me to grab it with a firm grip about 1-inch from the end. He said when you grab a stick, or any weapon, you treat the side your knuckles are on as the blade of a sword. As you swing the stick, you are slicing through your opponent using your complete body torque.

Next he taught me how to stand, and that the defensive stance was a relaxed but ready stance with your stick down at your side ready to block. Your feet should be shoulder's-width apart and you should be standing normally. He explained that you do not watch the stick, hand, or eyes, but use peripheral vision and watch the chest and neck area. The saying, "the hand is faster than the eye" is very true.

Another early thing I learned was how to twirl the stick. He then showed me some stick and hand exercises. He said now I was ready to deliver strike number one. After he taught me the first strike and I practiced it a dozen times, I was ready for the first block: the outside common. Since he was short and able to get in tight and low, Angel expected everybody else to do the same. I was about 5 foot 6 inches and around 97 pounds. He always stressed to stay low, ready, and balanced. At the end of each block, he would push my chest or shoulders to check if I was braced.

Angel made me do each block at least a dozen times each night we practiced. When I didn't have anyone to practice with, I would practice in front of a mirror or tall chair. He showed me how to develop speed and control, by striking at an object with a swinging stick at full speed so you could hear the wind, and than stopping it one inch away from the object, until you could do this without hitting it with your eyes closed.

Angel's classes at this time were not very strict. By that I mean that if you came in or left and forgot to salute, he didn't make you drop and do twenty push-ups. However, we were taught to respect our master by saluting him as we first met and as we left. He also taught me the proper way to shake hands with anyone. He said that as you shake with your right hand, your left hand should grab the other person's right wrist. This way the person would have less a chance of starting to shake your hand and then thrusting his right hand into your gut.

We started each class close to seven o'clock. We would stand in a straight line, or two if we had more students. Angel and Dentoy would stand in front facing us, and then we would salute. They told us who we would practice with and what number to teach or practice. We would practice for about an hour, take a 10- or 15-minute break, and then practice until nine or so.

One time, a student named Keith Scott was laughing a little too much while practicing. Dentoy was serious for the most part, and he went over to Keith and told him to punch at him. Being an obedient student Keith punched at Dentoy. Dentoy blocked and took Keith down to the floor. Keith got up and asked, "What was that for?" Dentoy said, "You swung at me so I had to defend myself, next time quit laughing and start practicing."

As I practiced, I got faster and started to flow with balance and control. When I was there, Angel had his class structured so that it should have taken about 1 month to learn each strike and all the blocks for that strike. Now, to make it through all twelve strikes and blocks would take an average person about one and a half years to complete Angel's system.

Rene Latosa,
Abel B. Miraflor,
Art Miraflor,
circa 1968.

The Miraflor brothers flank Dentoy Revillar.

From when I started, it took me 10 months to complete all twelve strikes. Now, that was not normal. Angel did not move you to the next level or strike until you passed when he tested you, and he felt you were ready to move up. Up to that time I was paying twenty dollars a month. Then, Angel said he would make me an assistant instructor under Rene Latosa and only charge me ten dollars a month.

Mixed with our regular stick practice, we did some kicks, knife, hand-to-hand, and stick-to-hand. Our kicks were never higher than our waist, with several outside and inside blocks. We did knife defenses against one to five strikes, including take-aways (disarms). Our hand-to-hand was real interesting, because when you were able to move the stick with a blur and have 100-percent control, when you put the stick down, your hands were three times as fast. Even to date, I feel my right hand is fairly fast because of this training.

Now, when you practiced stick-to-hand, you were talking about the real thing. That's when you had to really move and get with the program. I remember Angel always signaling me out to do "lock and block" or spar. On "lock and block," he would deliver any of the twelve strikes, following in between each strike with a number five strike with a short 12-inch stick in the left hand, thrusting at your gut. You talk about a workout! That and sparring could give you a cardio, if you're not in shape.

When I sparred, I got down to my knees, touching the ground, and drove you into the wall, going 100 miles an hour. Besides padded stick fighting, sparring stick to stick is the next thing to a real fight. You don't know what number the other guy will deliver, and it comes from all angles.

I remember another drill Angel would do in class. It was like lock and block, but with one stick; I always called it fakes. He would position himself as if he was delivering a number two, but halfway through his strike, he'd change and hit you with a number four. Or he would start out with a number three and change to a one. This type of drill is what really made you fast, proud of your style, and self-confident.

I was with Angel from late 1968 to 1972, when I was drafted into the Marines and sent overseas. Most people don't know this, but during this time, there were more masters and escrimadors teaching under the same roof at one time than at any other time in the history of escrima in the United States.

To the best of my recollection, there was Grandmaster Angel Cabales, Grandmaster Leo Grion, Master Gilbert Tenio, Master Dentoy Revillar, Master Max Sarmiento, and several other instructors that always came by to visit and see how the first public escrima school was doing, such as Art Diocson.

I remember Grandmaster Leo Giron coming in and showing us some of his *de fondo* style with a 30-inch stick. His wife would come with him and sit in the corner, on the left as you would come in the door to the class. She would sit and watch everybody, while crocheting and making gifts for other people. She was a very sweet person, and I miss her.

One of the most respected persons, and one whom I've always enjoyed, was Master Max Sarmiento. He just had a certain way about him that made you stop, listen, and ask questions. In my years at the class, I don't remember one time seeing a stick in his hands. He was deadly with his hands. He would move so fast and gracefully. He was over 6 feet tall and probably just over 200 pounds—the biggest Filipino I ever met. Yet he had a big soft heart, and would do anything for you.

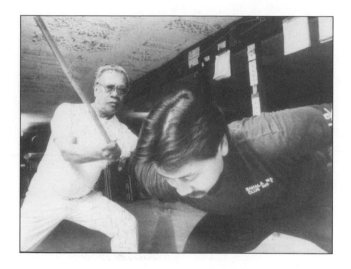

Grandmaster Leo Giron and Tony Somera.

For the most part Angel taught me at least 50 percent of the blocks himself, then I would say Rene Latosa taught me 30 percent, and Dentoy Revillar taught me the rest. My brother Abel and I would come to class every Monday and Wednesday and go home and practice almost every night. We loved what we were learning and wanted our dad to feel he was making a good investment. And he did.

Angel never taught us double stick, and the single stick was not over 24 inches long. The first hour of our class was normally dedicated to the stick, which was taught by Angel, and after break the last hour was for hand-to-hand, taught by Dentoy. We did not do any grappling, wrestling, or fancy kicks.

When sparring with sticks, we did not go looking for 18-inch short sticks; you used the same stick you always used. And when you sparred, you got as low as you could and used your arm, and swung using the full motion. By that I mean you were not allowed to just use your wrist, which is a lot faster, and that's what most people do now.

My experience with Angel was my first contact with the martial arts world, so my allegiance is first to Grandmaster Angel Cabales over any other instructor. I will always uphold his concepts and beliefs. A lot of people want to claim him, and step forward and use his name since he's passed on. But as martial artists, I think it is all our responsibility to carry on the arts and not speak negatively about someone who has passed on—or the same thing might happen to you.

This little essay I've given Mark Wiley describes my experience with Grandmaster Angel Cabales, and no one can change it or take it away.

May God bless all escrimadors in whatever good they do.

CHAPTER 5

THE UNASSUMING MASTER

By Rene Latosa

When I first walked into the Cabales Escrima Academy, I was greeted by an old family friend named Angel Cabales. He told me to grab a stick and hit him over the head. Tentatively, I swung at his head, and he proceeded to put an arm lock on me and took away my stick—all while puffing away on a cigarette. From that moment on, I was hooked.

Angel's training methods, back when I started in early 1968, were one-on-one. I was a very lucky student. Of my four years at the academy, my first year was the best. I was the sole student of Dentoy Revillar, Max Sarmiento, Leo Giron, and Angel Cabales—and I was not complaining. During some training nights, Angel would sit around and tell us about his experiences, while demonstrating each technique in the air. Angel never missed class, even during the harvest season. Angel worked for my father as a crew chief, and I knew his day started around 4:30 A.M., yet he would stay around the academy well into the night, teaching those of us who were interested.

Rene Latosa and Angel Cabales enjoy a meal.

My personal training with Angel was quite different from most other students. Angel trained me on the twelve strikes and associated defenses within a 2-month period because of the different events we were scheduled to perform. Every training class, I would be learning the techniques, while learning how to do demonstrations. All the training during that period was one-on-one because Angel believed that was the only way to learn and learn well. It was not until around my second or third year that group training was implemented. The group classes were never taught by Angel, because he still believed in individual training. He only agreed to groups because we started getting more students in, and they were getting bored waiting for individual instructors.

Angel always used me for weeding out those martial artists coming into the academy to find out what escrima was about or challenging the system. I remember one gentlemen who came in from a gung-fu style and wanted to know how we would defend against him. As he rolled around the ground kicking, I kept tapping him on the legs and lightly on his head until I had to do it hard enough for him to realize I was actually holding back. After that, Angel and I laughed about it and went out and had a smoke.

To me, Angel was just another old timer, and he never acted like the master he was. I remember being able to joke around with him. At a local Filipino event I saw him walking around, and I had not seen him for a year or so. I slowly snuck up behind him and made a mock attack to try to scare him. Angel just kept walking and asked me if I wanted to eat. He knew it was me.

When he had his class in my father's Filipino Community Center in the early 1980s, I walked into the class one day (after being overseas for several years), all 6 feet, 220 pounds of me, and stated to the person who wanted to know whether I wanted lessons, "Where is this Angel character?" I knew he wasn't in yet. So I sat in a corner watching the class. When Angel walked in, several students warned him that there was some big guy waiting for him as they looked over at me. Angel walked over to me as the class stared, and then we greeted each other and he introduced me to the class.

Rene later founded his own
"Latosa Eskrima" style.

It is truly unfortunate that Angel did not live long enough to realize that he has had a massive influence on the way Filipino martial arts are practiced today. Again, I was very fortunate to be able to experience one of the most valuable icons of the Filipino martial arts.

CHAPTER 6

A LITTLE ON LIFE WITH ANGEL

By Jerry Preciado

Training with Angel has been an experience that I could never forget. Angel was a great teacher and friend. He would never make you look bad and he did not care what color your skin was. He was there to teach you as long as he could trust you. As a child, I grew up with his family, since two of Angel's kids are married to two members of my family. Angel came to our home when I was just a kid, and gave a little demo for my mom, with two sticks. Everyone was watching him spin the sticks; he would get low to the ground, making the tips of the sticks tap the floor, making it sound like someone playing the drums.

When Angel was done, my mother asked him what that was called. As she held one of the sticks, Angel replied, "It's called escrima." Angel told my mother, "Since we are family now, your kids can learn how to fight." When my mom asked how much it would cost to have him teach us, Angel said, "No money. It's free for them to just come and practice."

Angel's two sons, Johnny and Vincent, became close friends of mine. They would take me fishing and hunting. They were both older than I was, since I was pretty young back then. I thought I was bad because I had learned how to spin one stick. As time went on, Angel would come over and pick Johnny and me up and take us to the farming camps to stay for the weekend. When we would first get there, Johnny and I would go in and switch mattresses with the old men, so we could have the thick ones, and they would have the flat ones. When they came back, the old men would get mad and blame each other and start fighting. We would beat them to the shower, since it was outside, and block the door with towels to make it a steam room so that when the old men would go take a shower, there would be no hot water left. It was a lot of fun.

When everyone would leave to go work the fields, Angel would give us some techniques to learn against a strike and then go back to work. We would be waiting for him to come back, but after about an hour, we would make sure he was gone and run inside the camp. The cook would be inside, and would feed us rice and meat from the big pots on the stove. Johnny and I would eat real fast and run back out like we had been practicing all the time Angel was gone. When it was time to go back home, Angel would tell us he was going uptown—where all the dancing and gambling clubs where located.

Angel always had a check in his front shirt pocket. Johnny would always ask, "Dad, what is that in your pocket?" And Angel would say, "Oh, that's nothing," and then he would feed us, give us five dollars, and send us on our way.

After Angel had opened the school on Harding Way, Johnny and I would go there to play, not to train. I already thought I could beat everyone up and if I couldn't, I would tell Johnny to do it for me. Johnny became another big brother, although I had four more brothers at home. I have seen a lot of people in my time, training in different places, and some do not remember me. I was the one who would just sit on the bench and watch them work out.

Jerry Preciado sparring with Angel Cabales.

In 1987, I started training seriously. Angel was not charging me anything to train. I had to make him take the money from me. He would say, "If you want to learn, I will teach you, and if you want to just sit, that is okay, too." He would never push you. It was a slow learning process, which took a long time to move on, because every time you came back to class, or on the next practice, you would have to start all over again from number one to wherever you left off. When Angel would see you doing the move the way he wanted, he would then let you learn more and that is one thing that made the art boring. But it made you remember so you would not have to stay on one number all night.

When we would have a break, Angel would tell us stories about when he was training, what it was like, all the battles he had, and the kind of work he did. Everyone would just sit and listen to him. When he would go to a student and show them something, everyone would stop and look to make sure that whomever he was teaching was not getting "more" than they were.

Everyone had a chance to workout with each other, and you were able to try out all the moves you learned. Each one of us had a favorite workout partner. You paired up with someone or you could trade partners anytime you wanted, which made a strong bond between everyone in the class. Nobody got hurt. It made you have respect for the other students that were training with you, but if you stopped coming to practice for a couple of months, Angel would say "Okay, you pair up with this student," because he knew the one he put with you would try you, just to make you feel weak for not coming to class.

And if you did not pay Angel, he would still teach you. He would look at you and say, "You pay next time." Everyone knew Angel was not after the money. He was after good students, ones he could trust. If someone from the old school came in and you did not know him, everyone in the class wanted to bang with him just to see how good he was, and Angel would just watch you beat him. It was like Angel would almost want you to show how good his new students were.

After receiving my advanced diploma, Angel asked me to start training at his home—in addition to coming to class—to learn how to teach all the new students that came in, and I did not have to pay for the class there. I was so happy to help him out, as he was like a father to everyone who was training with him. I had asked Angel how many master's degrees he was going to award. Angel said, "Just twelve, because that's how many students I had in my class when I was training." I replied, "I will wait for that one, number twelve." After telling Angel's son Johnny what number of master's degree I had, Johnny said, "If you want a lower number, you can have mine. I will just give you it." (Now I know what John was saying: you can have the diploma, but you still have to learn everything. In the end, Angel awarded sixteen master's degrees, because some of his earlier master-level students were no longer with him and he wanted 12 active master instructors.

Cabales awarding Jerry his "Masters Degree".

Then Angel came to the class one day, telling everyone that he had nothing to hide anymore and wanted to give us everything. He said "I always keep a little from my students, just in case a student wanted to challenge me." Everyone was glad he was going to show us stuff nobody else had. Angel started showing everyone who was left in the class by that time, hand-on-hand, reversing, picking, *reserrada*, sticky stick with frilly, *fraile*, and more. These were things I never had seen before. I knew something must have been wrong for him to open up to everyone, but all he would say was, "I don't need it anymore."

Angel told me he was going to do a seminar, and he wanted all of his best students to be there to help him. I took my video recorder and a lot of film, since he wanted to make a video of the last seminar he was going to do. He did hand-on-hand, stick-on-stick, and some reversing. He asked me to make copies of the tape and sell them. He tried to pay all of the students who helped him with the seminar, but we all told him to keep the money. We all knew he needed the money. I have the original tape and I made a copy for Darren Tibon.

Weeks later Angel made copies of the key to his academy and asked Darren and I if we could open and run the school, and he would come by there. We knew something was wrong. Even though Angel was getting sicker, he was still coming in with a hat on, making jokes, showing he had no hair, and telling us more stories and still trying to teach. And he was still fast. He told us the doctor told him he had the heart of a 21-year-old man, and not to worry.

Rey Tap, Jerry Preciado, Kimball Joyce, Darren Tibon

After Angel passed away, I still was teaching at the school with Angel's son, Vincent, trying to help him establish himself with the students, because most of the new students had never met him before, but knew Angel had kids. I started noticing students from the past coming to class who wouldn't come when Angel was alive. Angel had already told everyone for more than three years, not to trust some of the old students because they were like snakes as they wanted to steal his art and mix it up like spaghetti to make it weak. I tried to tell Vincent this, thinking we should be able to talk. After all, we had grown up together, I am the uncle to some of his kids, and I was the only instructor Vincent had there from the past at that time. But I think these former students had already talked to Vincent. Angel had told us he had already run off the bad ones once and hoped they would never come back. But they did.

When I was trying to give Vincent my support, some of the old students would come by and say they sure missed the place and Angel. When I would ask them how come they were not working out here, they would reply, "Who is Vincent? I never worked out with him before." I would tell them to just come back when he is there. But after the lack of understanding between Vincent and me, I had to pull away from his school.

Still having the need to train and teach in my blood while everything was still fresh, I started thinking of all the good times we had in class. I began discussing this with Mr. Lee (the owner of the building where practice was held). He asked me how come I was not over there anymore. I told him Vincent and I were having problems with the way I teach. Vincent would tell me in front of his class that I was doing everything wrong, and that his dad did not do it that way, and for me to do it the way he tells me to. It hurt me more then anything to think that after all those years of training, Angel had taught me wrong. Then I thought I had better look at all the tapes I had to see where I went wrong. If it had been anyone else that said that to me, I would have asked him if he liked to play, because I know Angel would never have done that to me. In the end, I was doing it correctly!

Jerry Preciado giving his support to Vincent Cabales (center).

So Mr. Lee told me I could have the school on Sundays to train and to tell everyone to come. After hearing that, I called Darren Tibon to see if he wanted to open the school with me, since things had gone bad with Vincent, even after we had told him we would back him up on everything because Angel wanted for us to make the art as strong as possible. After all, we were Angle's disciples.

You will hear so much stuff about diplomas. I have a lot of tapes; I can let everyone hear Angel tell you who has a master's degree and who it was that put the diplomas together for Angel (Frank Rillamas). The only thing I can say is if you think the masters out there aren't true masters under Angel, or that they know nothing, all you have to do is try one if you want to play.

CHAPTER 7

REMEMBERING MANONG ANGEL

By Carlito Bonjoc, Jr.

My name is Carlito Bonjoc, Jr., and I teach three different Filipino martial arts: the Cades-Lapulapu escrima with my father, Carlito Bonjoc, Sr.; the Talawan Largo Mano system of Master Roy Onor; and the Cabales serrada system of Master Angel Cabales.

In the summer of 1979, I was introduced to Master Angel Cabales. After seeing his system of escrima, I asked my father for approval to study under Angel. This was the beginning of my relationship with Manong.

At the start I was paired with one of Angel's advanced instructors. We immediately went into the defenses for strike one. This type of training is very effective, with true combat in mind, because of the way this system is taught, practicing the techniques while someone is striking. This concept is totally different from other systems that practice solo basics. In time, I improved, working with Angel's assistants and other students, and then reviewing with Angel.

I admired the fact that Angel had a keen understanding of the different needs of his students. He would teach each student according to his or her personality, physical makeup, and goal in martial arts. When I began training under Angel, my movement was good, but my balance was not strong. This physical challenge was the result of being born with my lower legs partially paralyzed.

Manong Angel looked at this problem and told me to come to his house on the weekends so that we could work to improve my balance and footwork. Angel put me through a unique training method that tremendously corrected my balance and gave me faster and stronger movement. This allowed me to excel, and I was then able to practice with the rest of my serrada classmates on equal ground.

Carlito Bonjoc with Angel Cabales.

In the eighties, I contracted a bone disease. This condition was not apparent until it reached the later stages and doctors told me that I would have to have my right leg amputated below the knee (and this was my strong leg). I became very depressed because I loved escrima so much, and I did not know what would happen if I was no longer able to practice this art.

Angel took me aside and told me that he would like to take me in a different direction. He wanted to show me how to break down the teaching methods, so that I could stay actively involved in the art by becoming a teacher. So began my training in this direction. This was the greatest gift that Manong Angel could have given me. By making me an effective instructor, he gave me back my strength and my focus. For that, I will never forget his kindness. Today I teach in Stockton, California, and I continue to promote the Cabales serrada system in his honor.

CHAPTER 8

TRAINING WITH THE GRANDMASTER

By Khalid Khan

I learned the serrada system directly from Grandmaster Angel Ovalles Cabales from 1987 to 1991, at his house on Cotton Court in Stockton. He trained individual students in the small front yard. I went there once a week on weekend afternoons. During that time, I had lost interest in my original career as an engineer in Silicon Valley because sitting too many hours in the engineering lab was not good for any masculine male's physical or mental health. I had no purpose at all in life, was not impressed with money, and had come to the United States just to meet people of education.

I met Cabales on the street one afternoon when I had gone to look for him. He took me to his house and straight away taught me counters for strike number one of his twelve-strike system. He acted like a host, and was brotherly.

He taught everything in perfection and completeness. His style was different from the other escrima styles. In the Cabales system you had to learn the correct stick positioning, hand positioning, and feet positioning, and had to do the counters at slow speed and perform them correctly.

Afterwards, you learned speed, reversal, and techniques, while doing the "lock and block" and flow drills. No other escrima system has his unique counter system, in which three subjects are taken care of: previous positioning of both sticks—yours and the opponent's—present encounter, and the next movements of both. You cannot disturb the balance of any of his blocks for any strike by adding or subtracting any motion from it, although, you do the counter up to the time allotted to it during a meet. Serrada has multiple capabilities between its counters. Serrada is never foolish; it always takes care of any next movement.

Khalid Khan

Serrada cannot be learned by all. Serrada has a major secret, which is very simple, and most people have ignored it. The secret is that you must do the first stage of serrada correctly, or "meaningly" (as Angel would have said in his English). You must learn the blocking (countering) system as Angel gave it. Afterward, this knowledge will help you produce the snap and checking that is seen in masters of this art when they demonstrate it.

I cannot ever forget those afternoons at Angel's house. I met Darren Tibon, Sultan Uddin (Kimball Joyce), and Jerry Preciado, and they also instructed me during some of the classes.

One night many years later, I was going on a street, and three men came into my car to kidnap me. They had brought sticks and a two-by-four wooden plank. The sticks they brought were longer than the serrada stick, which is usually less than 2 feet. I was initially surprised by such an attack. Then, I thought to myself, Let us take this as an escrima class. I approached each attacker and disarmed him, then I also hit their automobile with my own stick and dented it. They abandoned everything and ran. Soon, one of them returned crying that it was his father's car. But, by this time many people had gathered around me, and they ganged up and attacked me because they did not want any violence in the area. I learned that the human society is completely dumb and evil and will not support an innocent man when he stands up. I had to escape myself in a taxi that was passing by.

I learned the importance of mental conditioning. There is nothing to a fight. Human beings are all actors, and a fight is a geometry competition. Now, I stay away from the public in order to always know myself and stay mentally ready. An escrimador must be ready for any incoming strike.

Khalid Khan training with Angel Cabales.

Angel did not put on any airs of personal importance, but correctly defined his own position at times. You start understanding his system when you start doing reversals through your own acquired ingenuity. His style's most important defenses are against strike one and strike seven.

Angel Cabales' serrada system is now perhaps the world's biggest escrima style. I have students in Hong Kong, southern Philippines, Java, Malaysia, Sumatra, Thailand, Indian Ocean islands, Pakistan, Afghanistan, the Arabian peninsula, East Africa, Uganda, and Congo. I gave up my regular career for a number of years in order to be available to students in that part of the world. I also met visiting American and European students, who learned the serrada system from me in

Pakistan. I did not make any income but I learned a lot about how to instruct. My physical health and my vision about the future improved, and I thank God for making my destiny such a work. In Pakistan, at an academy that accommodated and housed war-orphans from Afghanistan and places like Chechnya and elsewhere, I met a big group of young people who immediately took to serrada. They practiced for a few years daily.

Cabales demonstrates the "shoulder" block.

Mark Wiley brought the art to Japan, Malaysia, and also to the Philippines. The other territories are taken care of by Jimmy Tacosa, Mike Inay, Sultan Uddin (Kimball Joyce), and other masters as well. But the style is not a mass-taught style, it is a one-to-one style. It exists as a secret martial arts cult, and you don't know any escrima until you do serrada. Nobody who had disrespect for Angel is on the bandwagon of this success and fame in places so far and wide on the globe.

I am proud of my association with Angel, and the instructions and blessings that I received in my life through meeting all of his senior instructors.

CHAPTER 9

THE ART AND SCIENCE OF SERRADA

By Anthony Davis

I first met Grandmaster Angel Cabales in 1984. As an accomplished martial artist in my own right—with 26 years of experience—I knew instantly that after having viewed Cabales in action that he was indeed a genuine weapons master. I was a private graduate student of Grandmaster Cabales.

What appeals to me the most about the art and science of serrada escrima is its simplicity of application. The empty-hand applications of serrada escrima are identical to the style's weapon applications, thus making it extremely easy for a person to learn. The footwork in the system is very fast and economical, and once properly learned and mastered, adds extra power to all of the techniques used in the art.

On June 3, 1990, I traveled to Stockton for the purpose of conducting a rare and close-up interview with Angel at his home. Although I'd had numerous conversations in the past with Angel concerning his system of combat, for some strange reason I was always reluctant to question him about the many duels that he had personally engaged in. However, I felt it was imperative that I extract this particular information form him. Cabales explained to me that he had fought in over thirty-five matches to the death. Some of these matches were actual challenges and the others were in defense of his life or loved ones. In other words, Cabales only killed out of self-defense.

Grandmaster Cabales explained to me that the art of escrima was never designed to be a sport, and therefore one must never injure another human being unless it becomes necessary. Cabales also explained to me that escrima death matches were an integral part of the ancient warrior traditions in the Philippines. In the words of Cabales, "To willfully test one's skills in an actual match to the death is the ultimate test of skill and courage." Grandmaster Cabales told me that the key to the success of all his duels was his personal belief that life is eternal.

Cabales instructing Anthony Davis.

Cabales explained that whenever you are engaged in mortal combat you must forget all of the antics of your opponent. One must not worry about things like how big or strong or how great your enemies' reputations are. One must remain calm but as alert as possible and strike the enemy down with accuracy, certainty, and power.

Cabales told me a story about one of his encounters that had taken place in the Philippines. He first looked around the room to see if his wife was present, and after observing that she was not, he proceeded to tell me his story about a medicine man who was from a particular village in the southern part of the islands.

Explained Cabales, "There was a very pretty girl that I used to visit whenever I came to her village town. One day while on my way to see her, I was approached by some men that knew me, and they told me with much fear in their voices not to try and visit my girlfriend because the village shaman had forbidden the young single women from dating all outsiders. Besides that, this same shaman was reported to already have killed two outside village suitors with the use of his magical powers known as anting-anting."

Cabales continued, "I never have believed in magic, so I wasn't going to let a tall tale stand in the way of me visiting my loved one. As I approached the village entrance, I was immediately met by the shaman who loudly shouted that he would kill me with his knowledge of anting-anting if I came any closer to him. With the speed of thunder and lightning, I whipped out my stick and cracked the shaman over the head with it. As the shaman fell to the ground bleeding severely from his head, I then asked him, 'Why didn't your magical powers block my stick?'"

Three decades have already passed since the time that Angel Cabales opened the first official Filipino martial arts school in 1966. Because of Grandmaster Cabales' early pioneering efforts, escrima schools are now flourishing all over the world. As Cabales once said, "Escrima was taught before the 1960s, but it was taught only in work camps, or in the backyards, but never to the general public."

Grandmaster Cabales was not only the first escrima master to open an escrima academy in America, but he was also one of the first Filipino masters who taught his art to non-Filipinos. Cabales emphatically believed that everyone had the right to learn how to defend themselves in times of danger regardless of their nationality. One of his special joys was working with young people because he felt they represented the future.

Angel Cabales after a seminar at Davis' school.

Though old in years, Cabales was young at heart. The times that made the Grandmaster happiest were when he had the opportunity to teach his special system of martial arts to others. Toward the end of his life, he began to realize that his ultimate dream was finally coming true: that his system of serrada escrima was gaining worldwide recognition as another classic method of martial arts that would live on through his students from generation to generation. Through the tireless efforts of Angel Cabales' students and close friends like myself, Mark Wiley and others, Cabales' legacy lives on.

For the past 12 years, I have continued to spread and to teach his knowledge to people all over the world. Recently one of my top German protégés, Uwe Guetschow, captured first place in the heavyweight division at the Eskrima-Kali-Arnis Federation IV World Championships held in Carson City, California. I have traveled in and out of Germany for the past 7 years in order to share Angel's knowledge with the people there.

If Grandmaster Angel Cabales were alive today, I think he would be beaming with pride and joy to see in how many positive directions his serrada system has gone.

CHAPTER 10

ESSENTIAL ATTRIBUTES

This is the first chapter that deals with physical instruction. Without an understanding of the essential attributes (i.e., proper body positioning and mechanics, the concept of distance, methods of footwork, striking qualities, and use of the checking hand) one cannot effectively apply a technique in combat. There would be no foundation from which to build, no substance behind the blocks and strikes, and consequently no integrity behind the techniques.

Body Positions and Mechanics

According to Angel Cabales, there were traditionally thirty-three postures taught in the decuerdas escrima style of Felicisimo Dizon. These postures included, but were not limited to, methods of holding your weapon while walking down a crowded street, how to sit on your stick to allow for quick access if necessary, and how to stand with your stick in an unassuming manner with both of your hands free for use. These positions were essential for the survival of an escrimador in the Philippines at the time of their conception. However, since many of them are no longer practical or useful in our contemporary society, they have been forgotten or discarded. What has been retained, however, are the body positions and mechanics necessary to effectively employ this art for self-defense.

NATURAL POSTURE

The natural posture is just that: the natural posture we assume when standing in line or walking, with our shoulders down and hands by our sides. Since this is the most "natural" position one can assume, and perhaps the position one will find oneself in if attacked, all of the defensive techniques in Cabales serrada escrima are learned and practiced from this posture. In other words, practitioners of Cabales serrada escrima strive to perfect their techniques from a position of disadvantage, wherein they are not "squared-off" with their opponents or in a fighting stance prior to the initiation of an attack. It is believed that this posture offers practitioners the ability to develop the realistic reactions, reflexes, and timing necessary to defend themselves when unprepared.

THE ATTENTION POSITION

The so-called "attention position" is used only when receiving instructions during class time or in other formal settings. It is a position wherein the practitioner stands "at attention" with his or her feet a shoulder's width apart, and the stick and arms intertwined, thus being non-offensive. This position has no relevant application in self-defense scenarios.

THE FIGHTING STANCE

This is the position that the practitioner assumes when "squared-off" with an opponent and preparing to spar or fight, and it is a variation of the strike two chamber position. To assume this stance, place one foot in front of the other, the distance of a natural step. The hand holding the stick is placed in front of the midsection with the stick in the crook of the elbow of the opposite arm, which is bent at the elbow with the hand placed over the navel (Figure 10-1).

THE LOCKED POSITION

The locked position is the final arm position assumed after the completion of a counter technique, wherein one is in a guarded, or "locked," position that is said to be impenetrable. This position one finds is basically the transverse of the fighting stance, since the left hand is held above the stick, with hand and stick moving back and forth in small motions (Figure 10-2).

10-1 Cabales in the fighting stance.

10-2 Chuck Cadell in the locked position.

USING PROPER MECHANICS

The techniques of serrada escrima are applied with speed and precision and with as little wasted motion as possible. All of the movements are condensed and solid—that is, with arms and weapon held close to the body, so as to reduce the chances of the opponent being able to counter them.

Any strike that is done with the mere extension of the arm is weak and considerably less than one that makes use of the entire body as a single functioning unit. A strike that is initiated from just the arm is only as strong as that arm, but a strike that involves the entire body is as strong as the combined elements of that body.

The power of the strikes derives from foot, hip, and shoulder rotation and from stomping. If the hips move first and the body follows, there is considerably more power and force generated than if just the arms or wrists themselves are moved. Therefore, the entire body must move in the direction of each strike and step so as to ensure proper body alignment and mechanics for power and stability.

Controlling Distance

Aside from strong fundamentals, one of the most important things an escrimador must develop is the ability to control distance and movement—both his and his opponent's. In terms of escrima, there are generally three defined critical distances, or combat ranges that all techniques are said to fall within. It is within these distances that certain techniques may be employed more effectively than others. It is also the ability to control these distances, or fighting ranges, that determines the victor of a bout.

A critical distance can be defined as any distance that has the ability to form a crisis, or threatening situation. In escrima this refers to any distance from which your opponent can strike you with edged, impact, or anatomical weapons. Offensive as well as defensive strategies must be understood, developed, and mastered in each of the three ranges in order for one to truly understand the art. Moreover, the *concept* of distancing, or combat ranges, must be understood because there is no set numerical distance between each range, or between opponents when in a particular range.

THE CONCEPT OF COMBAT RANGES

Combat ranges in escrima are divided into long, medium, and close, and are those distances between opponents that at once affect and determine the effectiveness of one technique over another. When developing an appreciation of combat ranges in general, it is essential to understand that they are not predetermined but relative. In other words, one cannot say for sure, for example, that "long range" is a distance of 4 feet from an opponent. Rather, the critical distance of each range is determined by the height of both opponents and length of their respective weapons.

Combat ranges, then, are not "set" but conceptual, and determined by such factors as the relative height of the opponents, the length of their arms, and the relationship of both typology and length of the weapons they employ. Moreover, and depending on these characteristics, it is improbable that you and your opponent will ever be in the same range at the same time. In other words, while you are in medium range, depending on the physical characteristics of your opponent and both of your weapons, your opponent might actually be in long or close range.

Let's now look at each of the three general ranges more closely.

Long Range

Long range is generally determined as that distance between you and your opponent wherein you can effectively strike your opponent's body with your weapon at full extension of your arm, but you are too far away to check his weapon or use your empty hand (if unarmed) to strike him. At this range, aside from evasion, the only options open to you for defense are deflecting the weapon with your weapon, deflecting the weapon (if a stick) with your empty hand, or employing a time-hit by directly striking your opponent's attacking arm or hand with your weapon while stepping or leaning off its angle of attack.

Medium Range

Medium range is the farthest distance wherein you are able to strike your opponent's body or head with the extension of your weapon. While maneuvering in this range, there is also the possibility that your opponent may also be at a critical distance wherein he can strike you with his weapon. It is as a result of this danger that the checking hand comes into play at this range. The majority of disarming techniques are also executed in this range, because it gives you the opportunity, with the proper use of footwork, to effectively take away an opponent's weapon while being in a position in which the opponent cannot strike you with his free hand.

In spite of popular belief, Cabales serrada escrima is a medium-range fighting art. This is evidenced in the concurrent use of the stick and checking hand during counters, and the insistence of Cabales that the exponent of his art not be so close to the opponent during technique execution that he or she can be struck by the opponent's secondary hand. Furthermore, the term *serrada,* as used here, refers to methods of "closing-in" or maintaining a "closed guard" while countering, and not necessarily "close range." Moreover, while many contemporary practitioners of the art use a short, 18-inch stick, the original length of the stick was between 24 and 26 inches—the length utilized by most medium-range escrima styles. And again, the concept of combat range is conceptually relative; so just because one might be in close proximity to an opponent does not necessarily indicate one is in "close range."

Close Range

Close range represents that distance wherein you can effectively strike your opponent with either the butt end of your stick or with either hand, in addition to locking or choking him. Cabales used to say that when in close range, one is a bit too close to effectively use one's stick to strike one's opponent. At that distance, he continued, one should drop one's stick and continue the altercation hand to hand. The empty-hand blocking and locking techniques of Cabales serrada escrima, then, are best utilized in close range. If one attempts to employ many of the serrada empty-hand locks from medium range, the elements of leverage and balance are lost to the opponent, who can use them to counter or "reverse" the locks.

Methods of Footwork

The effective execution of offensive and defensive techniques is grounded in proper movement and placement of oneself relative to an opponent. The control of distance and maneuvering to the opponent's blind or weak side are best accomplished through skillful footwork. In the Cabales serrada system, there are five such methods of maneuvering in relation to an opponent.

REPLACEMENT STEPPING

Replacement stepping is the core of the defensive footwork because it effects both body shifting and zoning in the same movement. With this footwork, you are effectively replacing your lead foot in an effort to change your position in relation to a strike, while not changing your relative distance from the opponent. It accommodates the philosophy that while defending against attacks to the left side of your body, it is better to have your right side forward, and while defending against attacks to the right side of your body, it is better to have your left side forward (Figure 10-3).

Although all replacement steps are based on the same theory of maneuvering along two sides of an isosceles triangle and replacing the lead foot at the apex, and although all employ the same general movements, there are several ways to perform the replacement steps, each depending on the type of attack and the practitioner's last movement.

To perform the basic replacement step, begin in either the fighting or locked stance, with your right foot on the apex of the triangle and with your left foot at the left base corner. Move your left foot to the point of the triangle, next to your right foot, and as it meets your right foot, move your right foot to the right base corner of the triangle. You have now changed leads and shifted your body to face an attack from the right. Perform this sequence again on the opposite side, and then replace your steps as many times as necessary to effectively defend yourself and end the altercation.

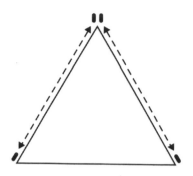

10-3 Replacement Stepping Triangle

A secondary method of employing the replacement steps is performed by first sliding back the lead foot a quarter-step followed by a full step with your rear foot before replacing your steps and lead leg. This variation is generally initiated from the natural position and is used when more distance is needed to effectively block or avoid an oncoming strike, especially when you have yet to achieve a "good" distance between you and your opponent.

CHAPTER 11

THEORY AND METHODS OF STRIKING

The weapon counter techniques found in many of the classical and contemporary arts of escrima are generally structured around a series of five, seven, or twelve strikes, commonly known as "angles of attack." And while these series of strikes are not looked on as attacking sequences or even striking combinations per se, they are used as a teaching tool, a method of ingraining reflexive responses to attacks that fall along clearly defined paths of motion, or "angles of attack." Cabales serrada escrima, like many of the classical systems, teaches its defensive techniques as counters against twelve strikes.

The Angles of Attack

The "angle of attack" method of learning defensive techniques is conceptual and makes sense in that there are countless ways in which one could be attacked, and to learn specific techniques to defend against each of them would not only be time-consuming but nearly impossible. By learning defenses against "angles of attack," as opposed to "methods of attack," the practitioner is able to automatically cover all possibilities of defense.

For example, the angle one strike is delivered to the left side of the head, neck, or collarbone. If someone were to kick you, punch you, or strike at you with a weapon to the left side of the head, why would you defend against each of these differently? On the surface they may all appear to be different; but on closer examination, it can be seen that they all move along the same path, aimed at the same target: the left side of your head. Thus, by ingraining in muscle memory various defenses against the angle one strike, you are automatically equipping yourself to defend against any attack moving along that same path.

In Cabales serrada escrima, the twelve strikes are executed in a classical sequence to preserve the art form (as illustrated here), and in a combative manner to promote effective striking skills. When classically executed (that is, with chamber and wind-up postures prior to striking), the twelve strikes form the nucleus of the Cabales serrada system. Although there are no prearranged forms in this art, the execution of the classical sequence can be thought of as such. Often viewed as a mere series of movements used to teach striking techniques, the classical twelve-angle sequence contains within its structure the entire foundation and advanced techniques of the system—such as footwork, stances, postures, hip and arm movements, striking and slashing techniques, blocking and deflecting techniques, disarms and reversals, punches, and strikes. If there is ever a doubt as to the proper placement of a stick, block, or hand technique, the answer can be found in this series of movements. Every technique can be proven correct or incorrect by referring back to the movements in the classical execution of the twelve angles of attack. This is perhaps the most important area of study, so it is vital that one learn these movements well and practice them diligently.

The Twelve-Strike Sequence

Although many systems of escrima utilize angles of attack, no two numbering systems are alike. Many systems have similarly numbered angles, and while the first five are identical, the remaining angles often differ, if only in their sequence. The Cabales serrada attacking system contains eight strikes and seven thrusts. Although this number of techniques equals fifteen, they are executed within the twelve strikes through combination and simultaneous movement.

The classical twelve-strike sequence is demonstrated here by Ron Saturno and JoJo Soriben in both front and side views. It is advisable to strike with the top 4 to 6 inches of the stick, because this area contains the greatest force.

STRIKE ONE: FOREHAND COLLARBONE STRIKE

Begin in a natural standing position with your stick held in your right hand (Figure 11-1). Chamber your stick by bending the elbow of your right arm until the stick is perpendicular to the ground and parallel with your chest, placing your left hand above your right hand and behind the stick, with the palm facing your body (Figure 11-2). Step back with your right leg, being sure to maintain the position of your crossed stick and hand (Figure 11-3). As you step forward with your right leg, strike diagonally down onto your opponent's left collarbone (Figure 11-4).

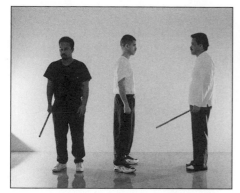

11-1

11-2

11-3

11-4

STRIKE TWO: BACKHAND COLLARBONE STRIKE

Begin in a natural standing position with your stick held in your right hand (Figure 11-5). Chamber your stick in such a way that your right arm crosses your body and your stick crosses your left elbow (with its tip pointing diagonally down), raising your left hand and placing it in front of your navel (Figure 11-6). As you step forward with your right leg, strike diagonally down onto your opponent's right collarbone (Figure 11-7).

11-5

11-6

11-7

STRIKE THREE: FOREHAND HIP STRIKE

Begin in a natural standing position with your stick held in your right hand (Figure 11-8). Chamber your stick by placing it at the side of your left hip (so that the tip points diagonally down), placing your left hand over it near your right hand (Figure 11-9). Step back with your right leg while horizontally moving your stick to your right hip (so that it is parallel to the ground and extending to the side) and rotating your left wrist enough that the hand ends up on top of the stick (Figure 11-10). As you step forward with your right leg, strike horizontally across your opponent's hip or waist, from right to left (Figure 11-11).

11-8

11-9

11-10

11-11

Strike Four: Sternum Thrust and Backhand Hip Slash

Begin in a natural standing position with your stick held in your right hand and a smaller stick or a dagger held in your left hand (Figure 11-12). While stepping forward with your left leg, chamber your weapons by holding your stick horizontally in front of your waist and placing your dagger or short stick on top of it a few inches from its tip (Figure 11-13). While leaving the stick in place, thrust the dagger or short stick forward at your opponent's solar plexus (Figure 11-14). Simultaneously retract the dagger while delivering a horizontal backhand strike across your opponent's hip or waist, from left to right (Figure 11-15).

When employing the stick and dagger, strike four will be executed as indicated here. However, if employing only a single stick, then the left hand thrust could become a punch or push, or the left hand movement could be eliminated from the sequence, and the movement thus becomes a solo backhand hip strike.

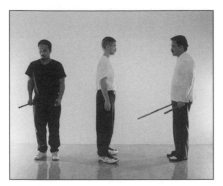

11-12

11-13

11-14

11-15

STRIKE FIVE: STOMACH THRUST

Begin in a natural standing position with your stick held in your right hand (Figure 11-16). Chamber your stick by raising it until it is both perpendicular to your body and parallel to the ground, placing your left hand palm down on top of the base of the stick in front of your right hand (Figure 11-17). Step back with your right leg, while either maintaining the position of your left hand, or sliding it toward the tip of your stick (Figure 11-18). As you step forward with your right leg, thrust the point of your stick to your opponent's navel or midsection (Figure 11-19).

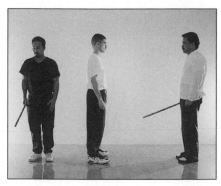

11-16

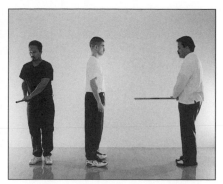

11-17

11-18

11-19

STRIKE SIX: FOREHAND SHOULDER THRUST

Begin in a natural standing position with your stick held in your right hand (Figure 11-20). Chamber your stick by raising it to mouth height, parallel to the ground and your body, placing your left hand behind the tip of the stick (with palm open and facing out) (Figure 11-21). While maintaining your weapon and empty-hand positions, step back with your right leg (Figure 11-22). As you step forward with your right leg, thrust the point of your stick at the left side of your opponent's chest (Figure 11-23).

11-20

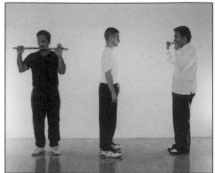

11-21

11-22

11-23

STRIKE SEVEN: BACKHAND SHOULDER THRUST

Begin in a natural standing position with your stick held in your right hand (Figure 11-24). Chamber your stick by raising it perpendicular to your left collarbone area and parallel to the ground, placing your left (open) hand on the outer-left edge of the stick, near its tip (Figure 11-25). While maintaining your weapon and empty-hand positions, step forward with your right leg (Figure 11-26). Thrust the point of your stick at the right side of your opponent's chest (Figure 11-27).

11-24

11-25

11-26

11-27

STRIKE EIGHT: DIRECT CHEST STRIKE

Begin in a natural standing position with your stick held in your right hand (Figure 11-28). Chamber your stick by raising it to chest height and holding it parallel to the floor with your left (open) hand placed in front of it (Figure 11-29). As you step forward with your right leg, strike directly at your opponent's chest, almost like a jab strike (Figure 11-33).

11-28

11-29

11-30

STRIKE NINE: BACKHAND STRIKE FROM KNEE TO SHOULDER

Begin in a natural standing position with your stick held in your right hand (Figure 11-31). Chamber your stick by placing it at the side of your left hip (so that the tip points diagonally down), placing your left hand over it near your right hand (Figure 11-32). As you step forward with your right leg, simultaneously retract your left hand to your chest while delivering an upward diagonal strike from your opponent's right knee (Figure 11-33) to his left shoulder (Figure 11-34).

11-31

11-32

11-33

11-34

STRIKE TEN: THRUSTS TO CHEST AND THROAT

Begin in a natural standing position with your stick held in your right hand and a smaller stick or a dagger held in your left hand (Figure 11-35). Chamber your weapons by placing your stick horizontally in front of your chest and placing your dagger or short stick behind it a few inches from its tip (Figure 11-36). While making an umbrella-like motion over your head with your stick and dagger (Figure 11-37), step back with your right leg finishing the motion with both weapons held vertically in front of your chest (Figure 11-38). Simultaneously thrust your dagger at your opponent's sternum, while turning your stick until it is parallel to the ground (Figure 11-39). Then thrust the tip of your stick at your opponent's throat (Figure 11-40).

11-35

11-36

11-37

11-38

11-39

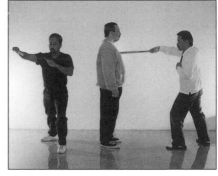

11-40

When employing the stick and dagger, strike 10 will be executed as indicated here. However, if you employ only a single stick, then the left hand thrust could become a punch or push, or the left hand movement could be eliminated from the sequence, the movement thus becoming a solo stick thrust much like strike 6.

STRIKE ELEVEN: FOREHAND STRIKE FROM KNEE TO SHOULDER

Begin in a natural standing position with your stick held in your right hand and a smaller stick or a dagger held in your left hand (Figure 11-41). Chamber your weapon by moving it over and behind your head, ending in a parallel position above your shoulders and with the palm of your left hand placed under its tip (Figure 11-42). Simultaneously step back at a 45-degree angle with your right leg, while lowering your stick until its tip touches the ground (Figure 11-43). As you step forward with your right leg, deliver an upward diagonal strike from your opponent's left knee (Figure 11-44) to his right shoulder (Figure 11-45).

11-41

11-42

11-43

11-44

11-45

STRIKE TWELVE: SIMULTANEOUS, DOUBLE CHEST THRUST

Begin in a natural standing position with your stick held in your right hand and a smaller stick or a dagger held in your left hand (Figure 11-46). While stepping your right leg back to reposition your body 90 degrees, chamber your weapons by making an umbrella-like motion over your head (Figure 11-47), ending with your stick and dagger held vertically in front of your chest (Figure 11-48). While stepping forward with your left leg, simultaneously thrust both weapons to each side of your opponent's chest or collarbone (Figure 11-49).

When employing the stick and dagger, strike twelve will be executed as indicated here. However, if employing only a single stick, then the left hand thrust could become a punch or push, or the left hand movement could be eliminated from the sequence, the movement thus becoming a thrust like strike 6 or 10. And if no weapons are used, strike twelve becomes a two-handed push.

11-46

11-47

11-48

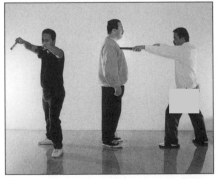

11-49

Striking Qualities

In addition to learning how to defend against a multitude of strikes, it is also important to understand and develop skills in how to strike an opponent in a variety of ways. If only one method of striking existed, there would be no need for self-defense, since everyone would know what to expect. Practitioners of Cabales serrada escrima, therefore, learn to execute their twelve strikes in a variety of ways to effectively make contact on their opponent. As a rule, it is best to consider the end of one strike as the beginning on another, thus keeping the flow moving and decreasing any "lag time" between blows.

STOPPING ON IMPACT

One method of executing a strike finds the weapon stopping on impact with its intended target. This method of striking is rarely done in combat, because maintaining your arm in any given position too long leaves it prone to being hit or your strike may be countered. (Although it is done on purpose at times to "set up" an opponent.) On the whole, this type of strike is used for training purposes, since striking and holding the strike at the point of impact allows your training partner to practice the correct form and positions for defending against a full-powered strike along that line.

FOLLOWING THROUGH THE TARGET

This is a full-powered strike that is aimed through its desired target. This method of striking does not stop until it comes to the end of its motion—unless it is met with resistance or is blocked—at which time it will continue in a different direction or change into another strike. A strike that follows through its target is best used sparingly, and as a "finishing" blow to end the altercation. If used too frequently, an opponent may be able to time your strikes, or you could inadvertently leave yourself open to a counter should you miss your target.

RETRACTING ON IMPACT

This method of striking involves retraction, which is useful when switching directions or angles of attack. At the point of impact, this strike retracts and switches directions to strike again at another angle. And while it is not a power or "knockout" type of blow, retracting strikes are often difficult to block, check, or disarm, and provide the ability to strike an opponent in numerous areas in a short span of time. This type of strike is the most popular among Cabales serrada practitioners because of its speed and snapping action. When done in combination, the retracting strikes become known as *abaniko* or "fanning" strikes.

Arcing and Circling Motions

Arcing and circling motions of the stick are seen in the majority of the basic stick counter sequences; here the stick is twirled in either an upward or a downward motion to block an attack and counter it or to strike the opponent in numerous areas. An important but often overlooked error when executing the arcing and circling motions is releasing the fingers. Although the looser grip may initially appear to aid speed, the power and stability of the strike is greatly decreased. Relax your hand but keep your fingers grasping the stick. With perseverance and proper training, you can perform this motion in the correct manner.

Training the Strikes

In combat, merely executing your strikes in the air will not suffice, because they will lack the power, stability, and intensity needed to end a confrontation. To develop these combative attributes you must develop impact power. One method of doing this is to have a partner hold his or her stick outstretched in one hand while you perform your various striking maneuvers against it. This method is only useful if you stand in the proper range in relation to the stick and do not "wind up" before striking, but strike from the block. Another method is to strike a heavy bag or post.

PART IV:

THE SINGLE-STICK DEFENSIVE SYSTEM

CHAPTER 12

BASIC BLOCKS AND COUNTERS

There are dozens of single-stick counter techniques in Cabales serrada escrima. In general, they are based around ten primary defensive techniques, consisting of eight stick-to-stick blocks and two empty-hand parrying/passing maneuvers. In theory, any potential attack can be deflected or passed using one of these eight defenses. In addition, the counter sequences follow a simple three-step pattern, beginning with one of the eight blocks, followed by one of four follow-up sequences, and ending with the "locking" technique. All things considered, while the defensive system is compact in terms of number of defensive maneuvers, its combinations and permutations are limitless.

Preliminaries

There are eight basic defenses used in Cabales serrada escrima. These include the inside block, outside block, cross block, roof block, umbrella block, shoulder block, punch block, fanning block, and an empty-hand parry and pass. The defensive method you use necessarily depends on the type of weapon you are attacked with, the type you hold (if any), and the relative position of your weapon to your opponent's strike. Each of the defensive methods is described in detail below, followed by examples of how to apply them.

THE CHECKING HAND

The understanding and use of the checking (or "alive") hand is one of the most important areas the escrimador must develop. Since Cabales serrada techniques are executed at medium range and in close proximity to an opponent, the skills and use of the checking hand are paramount and may be the deciding factor in life or death.

When employing the single stick, the checking hand is generally your empty hand. However, when employing a stick and dagger or double sticks, the techniques of the checking hand are generally performed by the less-dominant weapon (which is generally held in the less-dominant hand). In essence, the checking hand is used for supporting blocks, checking the attacking limb, disarming, striking, and passing or parrying.

The positioning of the checking hand is very important. Until it comes into play, the checking hand is held in front of the chest. The most common hand positions are with the palm facing toward the chest or facing to the right (if you are right-handed). In addition, when checking an opponent's weapon or attacking arm, it is important not to leave your hand extended for too long a period of time. By keeping the arm extended, you are in effect leaving it prone to reversal or attack, since your opponent may simply grab it, strike it, or even cut it. There is also a chance that you may inadvertently strike your arm with your own weapon. After an attack has been checked or countered, the checking hand must return to the chest area, where it can remain safe and ready for follow-up use if necessary.

THE "LOCKING" TECHNIQUE

The final movement of all counter sequences in Cabales serrada escrima is what is known as the "locking technique" or "locked position." It has nothing to do with a joint lock, but acts as a final checking or covering position used to end an attack while remaining prepared for another. The locking technique consists of three movements: 1) a check with your stick to the last position of your opponent's weapon, 2) a dagger thrust or empty-hand strike to an open target on the opponent's body, and 3) the "locked" or guarded fighting posture.

Inside Block and Counters

The inside block is one of the primary defensive techniques utilized in the Cabales serrada system. Since the angle one strike (a downward, forehand blow) is the most widely used method of attacking someone with a weapon, and since the inside block is among the safest and most reliable methods of blocking this type of strike, it is perhaps the most important block one must master.

In essence, the inside block is performed by stepping forward with the right leg (if you are right-handed) to move into medium range, while raising the stick vertically to block the strike to your left side, thus absorbing the force of the blow before it has had a chance to reach its full power. In support of the stick block, the left forearm is inserted behind the stick-holding hand, and the left hand is used to check the opponent's attacking hand or the base of his stick. With this method, your stick and checking hand act as a double defensive support system. After impact, the checking hand remains in place to "check" the weapon (hand), allowing you to counterattack with your stick with decreased chances of being struck by the rebound of your opponent's stick.

The following examples of the inside block are demonstrated by Frank Rillamas and Anthony Rillamas.

Against Strike One

This use of the inside block finds the practitioner blocking the attack and then remaining on the inside of the opponent's striking arm while executing the standard under-and-over counter sequence.

To perform this counter, remain poised in a natural position as your opponent chambers his stick to strike at you (Figure 12-1). As he commits his strike, step forward with your right foot and block his stick with yours at their midpoints (Figure 12-2). Slide your stick off his while checking his weapon hand with your left hand, thus safely chambering your stick for a counterstrike (Figure 12-3). While maintaining your check on the opponent's hand, strike your stick horizontally at his ribs or waist (Figure 12-4). Counter by retracting your left hand while striking under your opponent's wrist or forearm with your stick (Figure 12-5), checking the opponent's hand again for safety as you twirl your stick (Figure 12-6) to then strike down on top of your opponent's wrist or forearm (Figure 12-7). Finish by performing the lock maneuver by turning to face your opponent while lowering your stick and checking his weapon hand with your left hand (Figure

12-8), followed by striking at your opponent with your left hand (Figure 12-9), and ending by retracting and then extending your left hand and stick accordingly (Figures 12-10 and 12-11).

12-1

12-2

12-3

12-4

12-5

12-6

12-7

12-8

12-9

12-10

12-11

AGAINST STRIKE SIX

This use of the inside block finds the practitioner blocking the stick thrust and then maneuvering under the opponent's attacking arm from the inside of his strike to a more safe outside location, while executing multiple counterstrikes in the process.

To perform this counter, remain poised in a natural position as your opponent chambers his stick to strike at you (Figure 12-12). As he commits his strike, simultaneously step forward with your right leg, block his stick with yours, and place your left hand beneath his attacking hand (Figure 12-13). While raising your opponent's weapon, lower your body while striking your opponent's lead knee (Figure 12-14). Maintain control of the opponent's weapon hand while returning to a standing position and executing a vertical, backhand strike to his elbow (Figure 12-15). Maneuver yourself to the outside of his weapon by checking his attacking arm or shoulder with your left hand and stepping forward with your left leg, while positioning your stick in front of you for safety (Figure 12-16). Strike down onto the forearm or wrist of your opponent's attacking arm (Figure 12-17), and finish by performing the lock maneuver, using your stick to check your opponent's arm (Figure 12-18), and then punching his ribs with your left hand (Figure 12-19), and end by retracting and then extending your left hand and stick accordingly (Figures 12-20 and 12-21).

12-12

12-13

12-14

12-15

12-16

12-17

12-18

12-19

12-20

12-21

AGAINST STRIKE TEN

This use of the inside block finds the practitioner blocking the stick thrust and then maneuvering over the opponent's attacking arm from the inside of his strike to a more safe outside location, while maintaining pressure around the opponent's wrist. This techniques, while certainly effective with a stick, is more suited to a sword or long knife. When using a stick, the circling maneuver is used to maintain control of the opponent's arm, since a stick obviously cannot slice.

To perform this counter, remain poised in a natural position as your opponent chambers his stick to strike at you (Figure 12-22). As your opponent thrusts his dagger or short stick at you, rotate your stick clockwise to block it while also raising your left hand to chest height (Figure 12-23). As he commits his follow-up stick thrust, step forward with your right foot and block his stick with yours (Figure 12-24). Slide your stick off his while checking his weapon hand with your left hand and safely chambering your stick for a counter strike (Figure 12-25). While maintaining your check on the opponent's hand, strike your stick horizontally at his ribs or waist (Figure 12-26). Counter by retracting your left hand while striking under your opponent's wrist or forearm with your stick (Figure 12-27), then immediately placing your left hand on top of the opponent's attacking hand (Figure 12-28). Using ample pressure, rotate your hand and stick over and around your opponent's hand (Figures 12-29 and 12-30). Upon maneuvering to the outside of his attacking arm, immediately check his arm with your left hand, while chambering your stick in front of your chest (Figure 12-31). Strike down on the opponent's hand or wrist (Figure 12-32). Finish by performing the lock maneuver, using your stick to check your opponent's arm (Figure 12-33), and then punching his ribs with your left hand (Figure 12-34), and ending by retracting and then extending your left hand and stick accordingly (Figures 12-35 and 12-36).

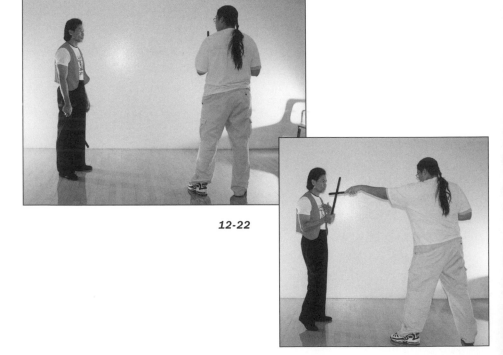

12-22

12-23

12-24

12-25

12-26

12-27

12-28

12-29

12-30

12-31

12-32

12-33

12-34

12-35

12-36

Outside Block and Counters

The outside block is another primary defensive block utilized in Cabales serrada escrima. When used as a force-to-force stick block, this defensive method is among the most effective defenses against an angle two (downward backhand) strike. When used in conjunction with the checking hand parry, the outside block can also be quite effectively used against a number of other strikes.

In essence, the outside block is performed by stepping forward with the left leg (if you are right-handed) to move into medium range to the outside of an opponent's attacking arm (whether it be his left or right). When employed stick-to-stick, the block is performed by raising the stick vertically to block the strike to your right side, thus absorbing the force of the blow before it has had a chance to reach its full power. In support of the stick block, the left hand is used to check the forearm of the opponent's attacking arm. With this method, your stick and checking hand act as a double defensive support system. After impact, the checking hand remains in place to "check" the attacking arm, allowing you to counterattack with your stick with a decreased chance of being struck by the rebound of your opponent's stick.

When employed in conjunction with your checking hand parry, your left hand actually moves the strike over your head, while the stick is used to strike the opponent's wrist, ending in the outside block position.

The following examples of the outside block are demonstrated by Anthony Davis and Ron Saturno.

Against Strike One

This use of the outside block finds the practitioner maneuvering to the outside of the opponent's attacking arm by using the left hand to parry the weapon or arm to the right and then flipping the stick up to strike the outside of the opponent's wrist or hand, followed by the standard downward counter and locking sequence.

To perform this counter, remain poised in a natural position as your opponent chambers his stick to strike at you (Figure 12-37). As he commits his strike, simultaneously step forward with your left leg while parrying his hand or the base of his stick with your left hand and chambering your stick for a counterstrike (Figure 12-38). As the opponent's stick passes over your head, simultaneously retract your left hand while striking his wrist or hand with your stick (Figure 12-39). Step back slightly with your right leg to adjust your position, while checking the opponent's arm with your left hand (Figure 12-40). Follow this by striking down on his weapon hand with your stick (Figure 12-41). Finish by performing the lock maneuver, using your stick to check your opponent's arm (Figure 12-42), and then retracting your hand and extending your stick accordingly (Figure 12-43).

12-37

12-38

12-39

12-40

12-41

12-42

12-43

AGAINST STRIKE TWO

This use of the outside block finds the practitioner blocking the attack stick to stick and remaining on the outside of the opponent's striking arm while executing the standard downward counter and locking sequence.

To perform this counter, remain poised in a natural position as your opponent chambers his stick to strike at you (Figure 12-44). As he commits his strike, simultaneously step forward with your left leg and block the opponent's stick with your stick, while checking his forearm with your left hand (Figure 12-45). As the opponent's stick rebounds off your stick, go with the force and push his arm away with your left hand to create enough space to safely chamber your stick for a counterstrike (Figure 12-46). As you retract your left hand, immediately strike down on the opponent's wrist, hand, or forearm with your stick (Figure 12-47). Finish by performing the lock maneuver, using your stick to check your opponent's arm (Figure 12-48), then thrusting at his ribs with your left hand (Figure 12-49), and ending by retracting and then extending your left hand and stick accordingly (Figure 12-50).

12-44

12-45

12-46

12-47

12-48

12-49

12-50

Against Strike Six

This use of the outside block finds the practitioner maneuvering to the outside of the opponent's attacking arm by using the left hand to parry the weapon or arm to the right and then thrusting the stick to the opponent's midsection, followed by the standard downward counter and locking sequence.

12-51

To perform this counter, remain poised in a natural position as your opponent chambers his stick to strike at you (Figure 12-51). As he commits his stick thrust, step forward with your left leg while simultaneously parrying his hand or the base of his stick with your left hand (Figure 12-52) and thrusting your stick into his midsection (Figure 12-53). Immediately raise your stick hand to check the opponent's weapon hand with the back of your weapon hand (Figure 12-54), then reposition your body while checking his arm with your left hand to chamber your stick for a counterstrike (Figure 12-55). Then strike down on his attacking arm with your stick (Figure 12-56). Finish by performing the lock maneuver, using your stick to check your opponent's arm (Figure 12-57), then thrusting at his ribs with your left hand (Figure 12-58), and ending by retracting and then extending your left hand and stick accordingly (Figure 12-59).

12-52

12-53

12-54

12-55

12-56

12-57

12-58

12-59

AGAINST STRIKE TWELVE

This use of the outside block finds the practitioner maneuvering to the outside of the opponent's attacking arms by using the left hand to parry the weapon or arm to the right and then flipping the stick up to strike the outside of the opponent's wrist or hand, followed by the standard downward counter and locking sequence.

12-60

To perform this counter, remain poised in a natural position as your opponent chambers his stick to strike at you (Figure 12-60). As he commits his double thrusts, simultaneously step forward with your left leg while parrying his stick with your left hand (Figure 12-61) and executing a horizontal stick strike to his midsection (Figure 12-62). Immediately raise your stick hand to check the opponent's weapon hand with the back of your weapon hand (Figure 12-63), then reposition your body while checking his arm with your left hand to chamber your stick for a counterstrike (Figure 12-64). Strike down on his attacking hand with your stick (Figure 12-65). Finish by performing the lock maneuver, using your stick to check your opponent's arm (Figure 12-66), then thrusting at his ribs with your left hand (Figure 12- 67), and ending by retracting and then extending your left hand and stick accordingly (Figure 12-68).

12-61

12-62

12-63

12-64

12-65

12-66

12-67

12-68

Cross Block and Counters

The cross block is so-named because on impact the practitioner's stick and checking hand and the opponent's stick form a cross shape. This block is quite strong, and finds your stick stopping or redirecting the force of the opponent's stick while your checking hand "catches" the opponent's attacking hand.

In essence, the cross block is performed against overhead strikes by stepping forward with the right leg (if you are right-handed) to move in to medium range, while raising the stick vertically to block the strike to your left side, thus absorbing the force of the blow before it has had a chance to reach its full power. In support of the stick block, the left hand is inserted in front of the stick-holding hand and is used to check the opponent's attacking hand or base of his stick. With this method, your stick and checking hand act as a double defensive support system. After impact, your crossed stick and checking hand together redirect the opponent's stick to your left side. Against horizontal strikes, the cross block is either used to block and redirect or to block and absorb the oncoming strike.

The following examples of the cross block are demonstrated by Art Miraflor and Rey Tap.

Against Strike One

This use of the cross block finds the practitioner stepping forward with his right foot and blocking underneath the opponent's strike—thus absorbing its force before it has had a chance to reach its full power—and redirecting it to the left before counterattacking with the standard under-and-over counter sequence.

To perform this counter, remain poised in a natural position as your opponent chambers his stick to strike at you (Figure 12-69). As he commits his strike, simultaneously step forward with your right leg while blocking the base of his stick with the base of yours and catching his hand in your left hand (Figure 12-70). On impact, and with your stick and empty-hand still in position, guide the opponent's stick down and to your left side (Figure 12-71). While maintaining your left-hand check, simultaneously push the opponent's arm away from your body while striking diagonally down on his inner forearm with your stick (Figure 12-72), ending in a frontal chamber position (Figure 12-73) wherein your stick points toward the opponent, thus keeping him from rushing in. Counter by retracting your left hand while striking under your opponent's wrist or forearm with your stick (Figure 12-74), twirling your stick (Figure 12-75) to then strike down on top of your opponent's wrist or forearm (Figure 12-76). Finish by performing the lock maneuver by turning to face your opponent while lowering your stick and checking his weapon hand with your left hand (Figure 12-77), followed by extending and then retracting your weapon (Figures 12-78 and 12-79).

12-69

12-70

12-71

12-72

12-73

12-74

12-75

12-76

12-77

12-78

12-79

AGAINST STRIKE THREE

This use of the cross block finds the practitioner blocking the oncoming strike and then maneuvering over the opponent's attacking arm from the inside of his strike to a more safe outside location, before finishing with the downward strike and locking sequence.

To perform this counter, remain poised in a natural position as your opponent chambers his stick to strike at you (Figure 12-80). As he commits his strike, step forward with your right foot and simultaneously block his stick with yours while checking his hand with your left hand (Figure 12-81). While maintaining your left-hand check, simultaneously push the opponent's arm away from your body while striking diagonally down on his inner forearm with your stick (Figure 12-82), ending in a frontal chamber position (Figure 12-83) wherein your stick points toward the opponent, thus keeping him from rushing in. Counter by retracting your left hand while striking under your opponent's wrist or forearm with your stick (Figure 12-84), and by immediately placing your left hand on top of the opponent's attacking hand (Figure 12-85). Using ample pressure, rotate your hand and stick over and around your opponent's hand (Figure 12-86). Upon maneuvering to the outside, immediately check his arm with your left hand, while chambering your stick in front of your chest (Figure 12-87) and then striking down on the opponent's hand or wrist (Figure 12-88). Finish by performing the lock maneuver, using your stick to check your opponent's arm (Figure 12-89), then punching forward with your left hand (Figure 12-90), and ending by retracting your hand and extending your stick (Figure 12-91).

12-80   *12-81*

12-82

12-83

12-84

12-85

12-86

12-87

12-88

12-89

12-90

12-91

AGAINST STRIKE FIVE

This use of the cross block is known as a "soft" defense, in that it does not require force-to-force impact. With this application, the practitioner simultaneously steps back with his left leg while raising his stick and checking hand to contact and redirect the opponent's stick thrust.

To perform this counter, remain poised in a natural position as your opponent chambers his stick to strike at you (Figure 12-92). As his thrust nears, slide your right leg back while guiding his weapon to your side with your crossed stick and hand (Figure 12-93). While maintaining your left-hand check, simultaneously push the opponent's arm away from your body while striking diagonally down on his inner forearm with your stick (Figure 12-94), ending in a frontal chamber position (Figure 12-95). Counter by retracting your left hand while striking under your opponent's wrist or forearm with your stick (Figure 12-96), checking the opponent's hand again for safety as you twirl your stick (Figure 12-97) to then strike down on top of your opponent's wrist or forearm (Figure 12-98). Finish by performing the lock maneuver by turning to face your opponent while lowering your stick and checking his weapon hand with your left hand (Figure 12-99), followed by striking at your opponent with your left hand (Figure 12-100), and ending by retracting your left hand and placing your stick between you and your opponent (Figure 12-101).

12-92

12-93

12-94

12-95

12-96

12-97

12-98

12-99

12-100

12-101

Roof Block and Counters

The roof block is so-named because the position of the stick when blocking resembles the crossbeam of the Philippine thatched roof. It is a block used to defend against powerful, overhead blows.

In essence, the roof block is performed by stepping forward with the right leg (if you are right-handed) to move into medium range, while raising the stick horizontally and parallel to the ground to block the opponent's stick as your left hand "catches" the opponent's attacking hand. On impact, your stick and checking hand separate, at which point your left hand maintains its check on the opponent's weapon hand while your stick is used for counterattack.

The following examples of the roof block are demonstrated by Frank Rillamas and Anthony Davis.

Against Strike One

This use of the roof block finds the practitioner blocking the attack and then remaining on the inside of the opponent's striking arm while executing the standard under-and-over counter sequence.

To perform this counter, remain poised in a natural position as your opponent chambers his stick to strike at you (Figure 12-102). As he commits his strike, simultaneously step forward with your right leg while blocking the base of his stick with the base of yours and catching his hand in your left hand (Figure 12-103). On impact, separate your stick and left hand, using your left hand to check his weapon-hand and create distance (Figure 12-104). Counter by retracting your left hand while striking under your opponent's wrist or forearm with your stick (Figure 12-105), checking the opponent's hand again for safety as you twirl your stick (Figure 12-106) to then strike down on top of your

12-102

12-103

opponent's wrist or forearm (Figure 12-107). Finish by performing the lock maneuver by lowering your stick and checking his weapon hand with your left hand (Figure 12-108), followed by striking at your opponent with your left hand (Figure 12-109).

12-104

12-105

12-106

12-107

12-108

12-109

AGAINST STRIKE TWO

This use of the roof block finds the practitioner blocking the attack and then remaining on the inside of the opponent's striking arm while executing the standard under-and-over counter sequence.

To perform this counter, remain poised in a natural position as your opponent chambers his stick to strike at you (Figure 12-110). As he commits his strike, simultaneously step forward at a 45-degree angle with your right leg, while blocking the base of his stick with the base of yours and catching his hand in your left hand (Figure 12-111). On impact, allow the opponent's stick to go with its force by separating your stick and left hand (Figure 12-112). Counter by retracting your left hand while striking under your opponent's wrist or forearm with your stick (Figure 12-113), checking the opponent's hand again for safety as you twirl your stick (Figure 12-114) to then strike down on top of your opponent's wrist or forearm (Figure 12-115). Finish by performing the lock maneuver by lowering your stick and checking his weapon hand (should it remain in place) with your left hand (Figure 12-116), followed by striking at your opponent with your left hand (Figure 12-117).

12-110

12-111

12-112

12-113

12-114

12-115

12-116

12-117

AGAINST STRIKE SIX

This use of the roof block finds the practitioner blocking the attack and then remaining on the inside of the opponent's striking arm while executing the standard under-and-over counter sequence.

To perform this counter, remain poised in a natural position as your opponent chambers his stick to strike at you (Figure 12-118). As he commits his stick thrust, simultaneously step forward with your right leg while blocking under his stick with yours and checking his hand in your left hand (Figure 12-119). On impact, separate your stick and left hand, using your left hand to check his weapon hand and create distance (Figure 12-120). Counter by retracting your left hand while striking under your opponent's wrist or forearm with your stick (Figure 12-121), checking the opponent's hand again for safety as you twirl your stick (Figure 12-122) to then strike down on top of your opponent's wrist or forearm (Figure 12-123). Finish by performing the lock maneuver by lowering your stick and checking his weapon hand (should it remain in place) with your left hand (Figure 12-124), followed by striking at your opponent with your left hand (Figure 12-125).

12-118

12-119

12-120

12-121

12-122

12-123

12-124

12-125

Umbrella Block and Counters

The umbrella block is so-named because the position of the stick when blocking resembles an open umbrella covering the head. It is similar to both the roof block and cross block, differing in that your stick and checking hand describe an umbrella-shaped motion over or in front of your head. It is a block used to defend against powerful, overhead blows.

In essence, the umbrella block is performed against overhead strikes by stepping forward with the right leg (if you are right-handed) to move into medium range, while raising the stick vertically to block the strike. In support of the stick block, the left hand is inserted in front of the stick-holding hand and is used to check the opponent's attacking hand or the base of his stick. On impact, your left hand moves to the left and your stick moves to your right, both describing the outer-top arc of an umbrella.

The following examples of the umbrella block are demonstrated by Jerry Preciado and Michael Keyes.

AGAINST STRIKE ONE

This use of the umbrella block finds the practitioner stepping forward to close the distance between himself and his opponent, while raising his stick and checking hand above his head to block and redirect the opponent's blow before it has had a chance to reach its full power potential. The block is followed by the standard under-and-over counterstriking sequence.

To perform this counter, remain poised in a natural position as your opponent chambers his stick to strike at you (Figure 12-126). As he commits his stick strike, simultaneously step forward with your right leg while blocking under his stick with yours and checking his hand with your left hand (Figure 12-127). On impact, separate your stick and left hand, using your left hand to check his weapon hand and create distance between you (Figure 12-128). Counter by retracting your left hand while striking under your opponent's wrist or forearm with your stick (Figure 12-129), checking the opponent's hand again for safety as you twirl your stick (Figure 12-130) to then strike down on top of your opponent's wrist or fore-arm (Figure 12-131). Finish by performing the lock maneuver by lowering your stick and checking his weapon hand (should it remain in place) with your left hand (Figure 12-132), followed by striking at your opponent with your left hand (Figure 12-133).

12-126

12-127

12-128

12-129

12-130

12-131

12-132   *12-133*

Against Strike Two

This use of the umbrella block finds the practitioner stepping forward to close the distance between himself and his opponent while raising his stick and checking hand above his head to block and redirect the blow before it has had a chance to reach its full power. The block is followed by the standard under-and-over counter-striking sequence.

To perform this counter, remain poised in a natural position as your opponent chambers his stick to strike at you (Figure 12-134). As he commits his stick strike, simultaneously step forward with your right leg while blocking under his stick with yours and checking his hand in your left hand (Figure 12-135). On impact, separate your stick and left hand, using your left hand to check his weapon hand and create distance between you (Figure 12-136). Counter by retracting your left hand while striking under your opponent's wrist or forearm with your stick (Figure 12-137), checking the opponent's hand again for safety as you twirl your stick (Figure 12-138) to then strike down on top of your opponent's wrist or forearm (Figure 12-139). Finish by performing the lock maneuver by lowering your stick and checking his weapon hand (should it remain in place) with your left hand (Figure 12-140), followed by striking at your opponent with your left hand (Figure 12-141).

12-134

12-135

12-136

12-137

12-138

12-139

12-140	*12-141*

Shoulder Block and Counters

The shoulder block is so-named because the stick is held point down and parallel with your shoulder. Being one of the less stable blocks in the system, the shoulder block does not absorb the force of a blow. Rather, the left hand intercepts and retards the force of the attacking arm, while the stick acts as a cover to deflect the opponent's stick, should it rebound from the force of the checking hand block.

In essence, the shoulder block is performed by stepping forward with the left leg (if you are right-handed) to move into medium range, while raising the butt-end of the stick vertically until the tip points down to counter a strike to your right side. Again, in this case the stick is the support for the hand. Despite its frail nature, the shoulder block is a fast maneuver that allows one to block and counter quickly with an angle one strike.

The following examples of the shoulder block are demonstrated by Jerry Preciado and Michael Keyes.

AGAINST STRIKE TWO

This use of the shoulder block finds the practitioner stepping forward to close the distance and block the strike before it has had a chance to reach its full power. After the primary counterstrike, you maneuver to the inside of the attacker's arm to finish with the standard under-and-over counter sequence.

To perform this counter, remain poised in a natural position as your opponent chambers his stick to strike at you (Figure 12-142). As he commits his strike, simultaneously step forward with your left leg and block the opponent's stick with your stick (point down), while checking his forearm with your left hand (Figure 12-143). Immediately strike down on the top of his wrist with your stick (Figure 12-144), and then again on the side of his wrist by flipping your stick counterclockwise, while controlling his attacking hand with your left hand (Figure 12-145). Use your left-hand control to maneuver the opponent's arm to your left, while circling your stick clockwise to strike him on the underside of his arm from the inside (Figure 12-146). Follow this movement by checking the opponent's hand again for safety as you twirl your stick (Figure 12-147) to then strike down on top of your opponent's wrist or forearm (Figure 12-148). Finish by performing the lock maneuver by lowering your stick and checking his weapon hand with your left hand (Figure 12-149), and square off with the opponent in a ready position (Figure 12-150).

12-142

12-143

12-144

12-145

12-146

12-147

12-148

12-149

12-150

AGAINST STRIKE SEVEN

This use of the shoulder block finds the practitioner stepping forward with his left foot to close the distance between himself and the opponent to deflect the opponent's thrust before it has had a chance to reach its full power. After the initial block, a check extension and direct angle one strike follow-up are executed.

To perform this counter, remain poised in a natural position as your opponent chambers his stick to strike at you (Figure 12-151). As he commits his stick thrust, simultaneously step forward with your left leg and block the opponent's stick with your stick (point down), while checking his forearm with your left hand (Figure 12-152). As the opponent's stick rebounds off your stick, go with the force and push his arm away with your left hand to create enough space to effectively and safely chamber your stick for a counterstrike (Figure 12-153). As you retract your left hand, immediately strike down on the opponent's wrist, hand, or forearm with your stick (Figure 12-154). Finish by performing the lock maneuver, using your stick to check your opponent's arm (Figure 12-155), and then thrusting at him with your left hand (Figure 12-156).

12-151

12-152

12-153

12-154

12-155

12-156

AGAINST STRIKE TWELVE

This use of the shoulder block finds the practitioner stepping forward at a 45-degree angle with the left foot to avoid both thrusts while raising the shoulder block to deflect the opponent's stick. After the initial block, a check extension and direct angle one strike follow-up are executed.

To perform this counter, remain poised in a natural position as your opponent chambers his stick to strike at you (Figure 12-157). As he commits his double thrust attack, simultaneously step forward with your left leg and block the opponent's stick with your stick (point down), while checking his forearm with your left hand

(Figure 12-158). As the opponent's stick rebounds off your stick, go with the force and push his arm away with your left hand to create enough space between you to effectively and safely chamber your stick for a counterstrike (Figure 12-159). As you retract your left hand, immediately strike down on the opponent's wrist, hand, or forearm with your stick (Figure 12-160). Finish by performing the lock maneuver, using your stick to check your opponent's arm (Figure 12-161), and then thrusting at him with your left hand (Figure 12-162).

12-157

12-158

12-159

12-160

12-161   **12-162**

Punch Block and Counters

The punch block is so-named because the action made by the stick hand when blocking resembles a downward punch toward the floor. This block is effectively used against horizontal backhand strikes and upward diagonal backhand strikes, because it intercepts the top of the stick and redirects it down and away from the practitioner. Moreover, since it is not a force-to-force block, it allows the opponent's striking arm to complete its motion uninterrupted, thus exposing him to a counter-strike to the area where his strike initiated. The punch block is also known by such names as "drop block" and "hammer block."

In essence, the punch block is performed by simultaneously dropping your stick, checking hand, and body weight on top of the opponent's stick. As the opponent's stick continues its path of motion, your left hand keeps a check on it as your stick remains chambered for a counterstrike, which is executed while raising your body weight to add force to it.

The following examples of the punch block are demonstrated by Frank Rillamas and Anthony Davis.

AGAINST STRIKE FOUR

This use of the punch block finds the practitioner dropping his body weight, stick, and checking hand on the opponent's incoming stick, then keeping it on its path of motion and countering to the opponent's open area.

To perform this counter, remain poised in a natural position as your opponent chambers his stick to strike at you (Figure 12-163). As your opponent thrusts his left hand (which generally holds a dagger or short stick) at you, simultaneously raise the ball of your right foot and vertically rotate your stick clockwise to block the strike (Figure 12-164). As he commits his follow-up hip strike, simultaneously drop your weight onto your right foot as you step back with your left foot to create distance between you, drop your stick until it meets and deflects the opponent's stick, while using your left hand to check and redirect the opponent's left hand (Figure 12-165). Maintain your position, but allow your left hand to guide the opponent's weapon hand away from your body (Figure 12-166). Counter by retracting your left hand while striking under your opponent's wrist or forearm with your stick (Figure 12-167), twirling your stick (Figure 12-168) to then strike down on top of your opponent's wrist or forearm (Figure 12-169). Finish by performing the lock maneuver by turning to face your opponent while lowering your stick and checking his weapon hand with your left hand (Figure 12-170), and then thrusting at him with your left hand (Figure 12-171).

12-163

12-164

12-165

12-166

12-167

12-168

12-169

12-170

12-171

AGAINST STRIKE EIGHT

This use of the punch block finds the practitioner dropping his body weight, stick, and checking hand on the opponent's incoming stick, then keeping it on its path of motion and countering in the opponent's open area.

To perform this counter, remain poised in a natural position as your opponent chambers his stick to strike at you (Figure 12-172). As your opponent commits his horizontal chest strike, raise your stick and left hand to chest level and then simultaneously drop your stick and hand until they meet and deflect the opponent's (Figure 12-173). Maintain your position, but allow your left hand to guide the opponent's weapon hand away from your body (Figure 12-174). Counter by retracting your left hand while striking under your opponent's wrist or forearm with your stick (Figure 12-175), twirling your stick (Figure 12-176) to then strike down on top of your opponent's wrist or forearm (Figure 12-177). Finish by performing the lock maneuver by turning to face your opponent while lowering your stick and checking his weapon hand with your left hand (Figure 12-178), and then thrusting at him with your left hand (Figure 12-179).

12-172

12-173

12-174

12-175

12-176

12-177

12-178

12-179

AGAINST STRIKE NINE

This use of the punch block finds the practitioner dropping his body weight, stick, and checking hand on the opponent's incoming stick, then keeping it on its path of motion and countering with upward and downward strikes.

To perform this counter, remain poised in a natural position as your opponent chambers his stick to strike at you (Figure 12-180). As your opponent commits his upward diagonal knee strike, drop your body weight, stick, and left hand until they meet and deflect the opponent's oncoming weapon (Figure 12-181). Maintain your position, but allow your left hand to guide the opponent's weapon hand away from your body (Figure 12-182). Counter by striking diagonally up from the ground through the opponent's chin or face (Figures 12-183 and 12-184), and then diagonally down onto his head or collarbone (Figure 12-185). Finish with a left-hand thrust or strike to his neck (Figure 12-186).

12-180

12-181

12-182

12-183

12-184

12-185

12-186

Fanning Block and Counters

The fanning block is so-called because its motion when blocking resembles the shape of an open handheld fan. It is basically a passing motion and follow-up strike made with the stick in a continuous back-and-forth (fanning) motion. The fanning block, which is also known as the flip block, is quite versatile because it can be used effectively against thrusts, horizontal strikes, and diagonal strikes.

In essence, the fanning block is performed by raising your right leg or stepping back with your left leg (if you are right-handed) while flipping your stick sideways or toward you to hit or pass the opponent's stick. The follow-up strike is made in the reverse motion, by flipping the stick toward the opponent and striking his hand, arm, or head.

The following examples of the fanning block are demonstrated by Frank Rillamas and Anthony Davis.

Against Strike Three

This use of the fanning block finds you stepping back with your left leg to create enough distance between yourself and your opponent so that the opponent's stick misses you, and you can effectively deflect the oncoming stick with your own stick.

To perform this counter, remain poised in a natural position as your opponent chambers his stick to strike at you (Figure 12-187). As your opponent commits his horizontal hip strike, step diagonally back with your left leg to create distance as you arc your stick in a fanning motion to deflect his oncoming stick (Figure 12-188), then shift your body weight forward and fan your stick to strike down on his wrist (Figure 12-189), and then fan your stick again to either strike his wrist a third time or, depending on his weapon position, use your stick to check his weapon arm (Figure 12-190). Finish by thrusting your left hand at the opponent (Figure 12-191).

12-187

12-188

12-189

12-190

12-191

AGAINST STRIKE FIVE

This use of the fanning block finds the practitioner stepping back with his left leg to at once move off the line of attack and effectively deflect the opponent's oncoming stick with his own stick.

To perform this counter, remain poised in a natural position as your opponent chambers his stick to strike at you (Figure 12-192). As your opponent commits his stick thrust, step diagonally back with your left leg to create distance between you as you arc your stick in a fanning motion to deflect his oncoming stick (Figure 12-193), then shift your body weight forward and fan your stick to strike down on his wrist (Figure 12-194), and then fan your stick again to either strike his arm a third time or, depending on his weapon position, use your stick to check his weapon arm (Figure 12-195). Finish by thrusting your left hand at the opponent (Figure 12-196).

12-192

12-193

12-194

12-195

12-196

AGAINST STRIKE NINE

This use of the fanning block finds the practitioner raising his lead knee to move it off the line of attack, while deflecting the opponent's stick and countering with the standard under-and-over counter sequence.

To perform this counter, remain poised in a natural position as your opponent chambers his stick to strike at you (Figure 12-197). As your opponent commits his upward diagonal knee strike, immediately move your knee off the line of attack by raising it and twisting your hips to the left, while simultaneously fanning your stick to intercept his and checking his weapon hand with your left hand (Figure 12-198). Maintain your position as you strike diagonally up to his chin or face (Figures 12-199 and 12-200), and then diagonally down onto his head or collarbone (Figure 12-201). If the opponent retains his weapon, follow up by planting your right foot forward and retracting your left hand while striking under your opponent's wrist or forearm with your stick (Figure 12-202), checking his arm with your left hand and twirling your stick (Figure 12-203) to strike down on top of your opponent's wrist or forearm (Figure 12-204), and then thrusting at him with your left hand (Figure 12-205).

12-197

12-198

12-199

12-200

12-201

12-202

12-203

12-204

12-205

CHAPTER 13

STICK DISARMING TECHNIQUES

Disarming is an integral part of the Filipino martial arts. In fact, although regarded as tertiary techniques, methods of disarming constitute a good portion of the curriculum of most escrima systems, including Cabales serrada.

Conceptually speaking, a stick disarm can be achieved in one of three primary ways: 1) by directly striking the opponent's weapon-holding hand, thus causing him to drop his weapon; 2) by creating a fulcrum and lever by securing the opponent's stick and pushing it over your secured stick; and 3) by immobilizing the opponent's wrist then forcing his stick past his wrist's natural range of motion, thus forcing it out of his hand. Although these are the three most common methods, there are literally hundreds of ways one can express and manipulate them.

It must be understood that disarming a stick with a stick is not the same as disarming a sword with a sword or disarming a sword with a stick. The techniques in escrima are generally transferable from weapon to empty hand and from weapon to weapon, but this is not the case all of the time, and disarming is certainly one category where direct transference of technique is not advised.

Indeed, there are many more techniques one can safely employ when attempting to disarm a stick than a sword, without the chance of severe injury. As an example, whereas one can grab an opponent's stick to effect a disarm, one cannot safely grab an opponent's blade to attempt the same. Moreover, where one can block using force-to-force and then disarm with a stick, one cannot do so with a sword. And where one can use the empty hands to parry an oncoming stick and to then guide one's own stick around it to create a lever to effect a disarm, one can neither safely parry an oncoming sword with empty hands nor safely insert a weapon around an opponent's sword.

That said, the following techniques are but a few examples of single-stick disarming techniques found in Cabales serrada escrima. Please note that disarming techniques, like stick counters, are conceptual. Thus, you should experiment with the techniques presented here against each of the remaining nine angles of attack to see which works best against which angles.

The following techniques are demonstrated by Vincent Cabales and Gabriel Asuncion. (For examples of other disarming techniques found in this system, refer to the first edition of this book.)

DISARMING STRIKE ONE

Remain poised in a natural position as your opponent chambers his stick to strike at you (Figure 13-1). As your opponent commits his overhand strike, step diagonally forward to the left, while parrying his attacking hand with your left hand and chambering your stick (Figure 13-2). Immediately follow the hand parry with a clockwise stick strike to his wrist (Figure 13-3), and then insert your stick around his wrist (Figure 13-4). Using the base of your stick as a fulcrum, turn your palm up to lock his arm as you place the palm of your left hand under his stick (Figure 13-5). Once his grip is loosened and his arm immobilized, use his stick as a lever and simultaneously pull your stick back to your chest as your left hand grabs the opponent's stick and uses it to check his arm (Figure 13-6). Finish by retracting your left hand and striking down on his wrist or forearm with your stick (Figure 13-7).

13-1

13-2

13-3

13-4

13-5

13-6

13-7

DISARMING STRIKE THREE

Remain poised in a natural position as your opponent chambers his stick to strike at you (Figure 13-8). As your opponent commits his horizontal strike, step back with your right foot to create distance while passing his stick with your left hand and inserting your stick under the wrist of his attacking hand (Figure 13-9). Using the base of your stick as a fulcrum, turn your palm up to lock his arm (Figure 13-10), at which time you can take hold of his stick with your left hand (Figure 13-11). Once his grip is loosened and his arm immobilized, use his stick as a lever and simultaneously pull your stick back to your chest and extend his stick in your left hand to check his arm (Figure 13-12). Finish by retracting your left hand and striking down on his wrist or forearm with your stick (Figure 13-13).

13-8

13-9

13-10

13-11

13-12

13-13

DISARMING STRIKE FIVE

Remain poised in a natural position as your opponent chambers his stick to strike at you (Figure 13-14). As your opponent commits his stick thrust, step back with your left leg to move off the line of attack, while simultaneously inside blocking his stick with yours (Figure 13-15). Insert your left hand around the outside of your opponent's attacking arm as you use your stick to push his stick down and toward him (Figure 13-16). The simultaneous opposing actions of pushing your stick forward while pulling your empty hand back toward you will result in the opponent's being disarmed (Figure 13-17).

13-14

13-15

13-16

13-17

PART V:
THE UNARMED DEFENSIVE SYSTEM

CHAPTER 14

BASIC BLOCKS AND LOCKS

Cabales serrada escrima is first and foremost an art of stick-fighting. The empty-hand system was developed and incorporated later to accommodate the American self-defense mentality, and thus is introduced after a foundation in single-stick fighting has been developed.

The Cabales serrada escrima unarmed defensive system is made up of four categories: blocking methods, striking methods, locking methods, and disarming methods. It is important for the practitioner to develop equal skills in all four categories, because one cannot effect a disarm if one cannot first block the opponent's strike and then lock his limb.

In essence, there are three blocking methods (c-hand grab, double parry, and x-block), five striking methods (straight punch, hammer fist, chop, knee, and front kick), sixteen locking methods (categorized as bent arm locks, straight arm locks, and body locks), and two basic disarming methods (ejection and retention).

Core Blocking Techniques

As with multiple weapon counters, the knowledge of a multitude of empty-hand blocks, strikes, locks, and disarms is essential to effective unarmed self-defense. And the choice of when to move your hands to the right or left and what type of lock or disarm to employ is necessarily dependent on your position and your opponent's methods of attack.

The following two techniques, demonstrated by Carlito Bonjoc, Jr., and Joe Gastello, are the core blocks of the system, because these are the methods from which the subsequent locks and disarms are derived. (For examples of other blocking techniques found in this system, refer to the first edition of this book.)

THE C-HAND GRAB

The c-hand grab is the cornerstone of the Cabales serrada empty-hand system, since all other techniques stem from it. This technique finds the practitioner grabbing hold of and immobilizing the opponent's wrist, after which an effective strike, lock, or disarm is executed.

As the opponent commits a straight right punch at your head, grab the outside of his wrist with your left hand and redirect it to the right (Figure 14-1). As the opponent then commits a straight left punch at your head, grab the outside of his wrist with your right hand and redirect it to the left (Figure 14-2). As the opponent commits another straight right punch at your head, grab the inside of his wrist with your right hand and redirect it to the left (Figure 14-3). As the opponent then commits another straight left punch at your head, grab the inside of his wrist with your left hand and redirect it to the right (Figure 14-4).

14-1

14-2

14-3   **14-4**

THE DOUBLE PARRY

The double parry is an extension of the c-hand grab. In this technique, the practitioner executes an initial parry prior to grabbing with the secondary hand. This method is somewhat safer than the direct c-hand grab, because the initial parry before the grab decreases the chance of missing the opponent's strike and getting struck.

As the opponent commits a straight right punch at your head, first parry the outside of his wrist with your left hand (Figure 14-5) and then grab the outside of his wrist with your right hand and redirect it to the right (Figure 14-6). As the opponent commits a straight left punch at your head, first parry the outside of his wrist with your right hand (Figure 14-7) and then grab the outside of his wrist with your left hand and redirect it to the left (Figure 14-8). As the opponent commits another straight right punch at your head, first parry the inside of his wrist with your right hand (Figure 14-9) and then grab the inside of his wrist with your left hand and redirect

14-5

14-6

it to the left (Figure 14-10). As the opponent commits another straight left punch at your head, first parry the inside of his wrist with your left hand (Figure 14-11) and then grab the inside of his wrist with your right hand and redirect it to the right (Figure 14-12).

14-7

14-8

14-9

14-10

14-11

14-12

Core Locking Techniques

As mentioned earlier, Angel Cabales introduced sixteen locking techniques into his stick-fighting art, thus completing its scope as a true self-defense art. Locking techniques are considered secondary, because one must first have the knowledge and skills to block and counterstrike an opponent before one can effectively lock and control the opponent or lock and tack the opponent down.

**Angel Cabales demonstrates arm lock
with neck chop on Chuck Cadell.**

In essence, one must first move off the line of attack, position oneself away from the threat of the second (combination) striking hand, and effectively block or parry and then immobilize the attacking limb before a joint lock or body lock can be effectively executed. And while this seems like a lot to do, it is at once necessary and quick, as all of these things can be done in one continuous motion.

Since the straight punch is one of the most common types of techniques one can expect to be attacked with, the following locking techniques, demonstrated by Darren Tibon and John Lile, are illustrated from this scenario. To become well rounded, however, it is best to experiment with each of these locks against various types and angles of empty-hand strikes.

Straight Arm Lock One

Remain poised in a natural position as your opponent prepares to punch you (Figure 14-13). As your opponent commits his punch, simultaneously step diagonally forward with your left foot, while parrying his hand down with the back of your left hand (Figure 14-14). Continue to move to the left and parrying his arm as you place your right palm on his elbow (Figure 14-15). Maintaining pressure with both arms, slide your left arm under and around the opponent's extended arm and overlap your left and right hands (Figure 14-16). You should now be to the side of your opponent, with his arm fully extended and locked, thus making him unable to strike you with his free hand.

14-13

14-14

14-15

14-16

STRAIGHT ARM LOCK TWO

Remain poised in a natural position as your opponent prepares to punch you (Figure 14-17). As your opponent commits his punch, step diagonally forward with your left leg as you as you outside parry and grab his arm (Figures 14-18 and 14-19). Once you have secured control of the hand, cross your right foot behind your left in an effort to move to his blind side while extending his arm (Figure 14-20). Once to the side, turn so that you are facing in the same direction as your opponent, place his elbow over your left shoulder, and pull down on his wrist (Figure 14-21).

14-17

14-18

14-19

14-20

14-21

STRAIGHT ARM LOCK THREE

Remain poised in a natural position as your opponent prepares to punch you (Figure 14-22). As your opponent commits his punch, step diagonally forward with your left leg as you parry and grab his arm with an outside block (Figure 14-23), striking his elbow with your left forearm as you grab his wrist with your right hand (Figure 14-24). As his balance is disrupted, extend your left arm to his head (Figure 14-25), to further upset his balance, and take him down over your left knee (Figure 14-26).

14-22

14-23

14-24

14-25

14-26

STRAIGHT ARM LOCK FOUR

Remain poised in a natural position as your opponent prepares to punch you (Figure 14-27). As your opponent commits his punch, do an inside parry (Figure 14-28), followed by a right-hand strike to the opponent's head to distract him (Figure 14-29). Maintain your left-hand hold on his wrist, while taking control of his elbow with your right hand (Figure 14-30). Lock the opponent by bending and raising his wrist while pushing down on his elbow (Figure 14-31).

14-27

14-28

14-29

14-30

14-31

BENT ARM LOCK ONE

Remain poised in a natural position as your opponent prepares to punch you (Figure 14-32). As your opponent commits his punch, step diagonally forward to the left, as you simultaneously parry his punch down with your left hand and place your right hand on top of his forearm (Figure 14-33). Use your right hand to pull his elbow in an effort to bend his arm as you insert your left arm under his wrist until it reaches his shoulder, and turn 90 degrees to the left (Figure 14-34). Once you have secured your left hand in place, drop to your right knee to take the opponent down, while securing your hold by bending his wrist with your right hand (Figures 14-35 and 14-36).

14-32

14-33

14-34

14-35

14-36

BENT ARM LOCK TWO

Remain poised in a natural position as your opponent prepares to punch you (Figure 14-37). As your opponent commits his punch, step diagonally forward with your left leg as you as you outside parry and grab his arm (Figures 14-38 and 14-39). Maintain your left-hand hold on his wrist as you insert your right hand under his arm and pull in his inner elbow (Figure 14-40). Using the momentum of the arm pull, lead his hand to the left side of his neck with your left hand and then, once there, wrap your right arm around his neck and grab hold of his wrist with your left hand (Figure 14-41). Use this hold to pull the opponent to the ground (Figure 14-42), and then execute a hammer fist blow to his sternum (Figure 14-43).

14-37

14-38

14-39

14-40

14-41

14-42

14-43

Bent Arm Lock Three

Remain poised in a natural position as your opponent prepares to punch you (Figure 14-44). As your opponent commits his punch, step off the line of attack to the left, while grabbing the top of his wrist and hand with your left hand (Figure 14-45). Using your control of his wrist, turn the opponent's hand back toward him, thus creating a lock (Figure 14-46). Step in with your left leg and punch his sternum with your right hand (Figure 14-47), then use his lost balance and your weight to bring him to the ground (Figures 14-48 and 14-49).

14-44

14-45

14-46

14-47

14-48

14-49

BENT ARM LOCK FOUR

Remain poised in a natural position as your opponent prepares to punch you (Figure 14-50). As your opponent commits his punch, step off the line of attack to the left, while grabbing the top of his wrist and hand with your left hand (Figure 14-51). Once the lock is secured, place your right hand to the left of his elbow and use it as a fulcrum (Figure 14-52). Take him to the ground by moving your right leg behind him and directing his locked wrist down (Figures 14-53 and 14-54).

14-50

14-51

14-52

14-53

14-54

Chapter 15

EMPTY-HAND DISARMING TECHNIQUES

It must be stated at the outset that if you are unarmed and face an armed adversary, it is best to run. There is no room for bravado in a situation that may lead to unnecessary death. If you cannot run, then you must do your best to distract the armed attacker, knock over or otherwise throw objects between you and him in order to give yourself time to react and reposition yourself to your advantage. If none of these option are available, then (and only then) should you attempt to employ the techniques of empty-hand self-defense against a weapon. And along those lines, the first order of business is effectively using your angling and footwork to reposition yourself and then (or simultaneously) employing the empty-hand blocking methods. After you have effectively blocked an armed opponent, it is imperative that you lock him at once. Before executing your disarm, be very sure that you have secured a firm hold on his attacking limb, and that you are well away from his secondary arm (which may also hold a weapon) before executing a disarming technique.

As a result of space limitations, this chapter offers a mere overview of the empty-hand disarming techniques found in Cabales serrada escrima. However, in order to illustrate as many types of disarms as possible, Vincent Cabales, Stanley Wells, and Vincent Cabales, Jr., have demonstrated here two techniques against stick attacks and two against knife attacks. Again, it is important to keep in mind that disarming a stick is not the same as disarming a bladed weapon. (For examples of other empty-hand disarms found in this system, refer to the first edition of this book.)

Angel Cabales demonstrates disarms.

Stick Disarming Techniques

DISARMING STRIKE THREE

Remain poised in a natural position as your opponent chambers his stick to strike at you (Figure 15-1). As your opponent commits his horizontal forehand strike, step back with your left foot to create distance between you, while passing his stick with your left hand and inserting your right hand under the wrist of his attacking hand (Figure 15-2). Using your right wrist as a fulcrum, turn your palm up and take hold of his stick with your left hand (Figure 15-3). Once his grip is loosened and his arm immobilized, simultaneously pull your right hand back to your chest and extend his stick in your left hand to check his arm (Figure 15-4).

15-1   **15-2**

15-3   **15-4**

DISARMING STRIKE FOUR

Remain poised in a natural position as your opponent chambers his stick to strike at you (Figure 15-5). As your opponent commits his horizontal backhand strike, step back with your right foot to create distance between you, while blocking the base of his stick with your right forearm and parrying the top of his hand with the back of your left hand (Figure 15-6). Maintain control of his weapon with your right arm while inserting your left hand counterclockwise around his wrist (Figure 15-7). Once his arm is locked, secure his weapon by pulling his arm in toward your body (Figure 15-8). From here, you can either maintain the lock or separate your hand to effect the disarm.

15-5

15-6

15-7

15-8

Knife Disarming Techniques

DISARMING STRIKE FIVE

Remain poised in a natural position as your opponent chambers his stick to strike at you (Figure 15-9). As your opponent commits his knife thrust, step back with your left leg to create distance between you, while parrying the inside of his wrist with the back of your left hand (Figure 15-10). Take control of his wrist with your left hand, twist it, and bring it in close to your body to keep the opponent from pulling his knife away (Figure 15-11). Once you have secured the opponent's hand, stabilize the lock by applying downward pressure to wrist with both your left and right hands (Figure 15-12).

15-9

15-10

15-11

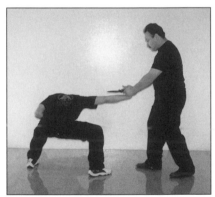

15-12

DISARMING STRIKE ONE

Remain poised in a natural position as your opponent chambers his stick to strike at you (Figure 15-13). As your opponent commits his downward stab, step back with your right leg to create distance between you, while parrying the outside of his hand with your left hand (Figure 15-14). As you redirect his stabbing motion, use your right hand for added support to turn the knife back into the opponent (Figure 15-15).

15-13

15-14

15-15

PART VI: TRAINING FOR COMBAT

CHAPTER 16

TRAINING DRILLS AND COMBAT STRATEGIES

The Cabales serrada system of escrima is characterized by fast, explosive movements rooted in acute reflex control and coordination. Practitioners train to develop the ability to strike with unpredictable suddenness. It is the attainment of this ability that facilitates the process of being able to defend against similarly deceptive attacks.

It is widely held that the hand is faster than the eye and, thus, one's vision will be impaired when pitted against an opponent who possesses a great deal of speed, fine timing, and deceptive feinting skills. In Cabales serrada escrima, such attributes are developed through responsive training drills and applied through deceptive combat strategies. Daily practice of lock and block, flow sparring, picking, reversing, and sticky stick drills and the strategies outlined below, will improve any practitioner's overall fighting ability and combat effectiveness.

Lock and Block

Lock and block is a training drill that does much to increase the practitioner's ability to effectively use this art in combat. It is a drill in which two partners face each other—one as attacker and the other as defender. The defender is armed with a long and short stick (or a stick and dagger), while the defender is armed only with a single stick. There are several levels to this drill, each building on the next, and each bringing the practitioner's skills closer to being actual rather than assumed.

Throughout this drill, the defender's goal is to block the initial stick attack, complete an entire counter sequence, and return to the "locked" fighting position held prior to the attacker's initiation of his knife or short-stick thrust. At this level, the attacker is striking along the twelve strike sequence in the following manner: strike one, dagger thrust, strike two, pause; strike two, dagger thrust, strike three, pause; and so on through the twelve strikes. This level is concerned with developing the practitioner's coordination and timing.

The next level of the lock and block drill finds the attacker delivering the twelve strikes and dagger thrusts consecutively, without pause, but this time not necessarily allowing the defender to complete each counter sequence. This level is concerned with developing the practitioner's timing and reflexes. Since the practitioner does not know if or when the attacker will allow him to complete the counter sequence against each strike, the defender must assume he can finish and is at times forced to parlay one counterstrike into the next block. Again, the end of one movement becomes the beginning of the next.

The advanced and highest level of this drill finds the attacker executing any number of strikes desired in any chosen sequence. Again, the attacker may or may not allow the defender to complete counterattack sequences. This level of lock and block is fast and furious, and in addition to highly developing reflexes, speed, and timing, it also develops the ability to move and react spontaneously without thought.

Flow Sparring

Flow sparring is a drill that develops the practitioner's fundamental skills in single-stick sparring. This drill initially finds its participants facing off and engaging in an even exchange of strikes and blocks. It is primarily employed as a tool to teach beginners how to block effectively and counterattack efficiently.

Flow sparring is initially taught in a prearranged sequence of movements to develop hand and foot coordination. The drill later progresses to a point where the strikes and counters may come from any angle, thus developing reflexes. In the latter stages, broken rhythm and feinting techniques are also employed in this drill, thus making it more realistic.

Picking

Picking (or faking) techniques are the icing on the serrada cake. "Picking" is a general term used within the system to describe the action of using deceptive strikes to open a target area that may otherwise be closed to an attack.

There are many types and methods of "picking," and each angle has multiple variations. Here, Darren Tibon demonstrates "picks" from the first three angles of attack.

Picking Strike One

When intending to "pick" strike one, be sure to chamber your stick long enough to alert your opponent to the fact that you are preparing to attack him from that angle (Figure 16-1). Allow your stick to move about two-thirds of the distance to its false target (Figure 16-2). As the opponent commits his defense (in this case, an inside block), change the angle of your attack and strike your opponent on his blocking hand (Figure 16-3). Immediately follow this with another change of angle (in the event that he is able to block your first feint), to strike his head or other unguarded target (Figure 16-4).

16-1

16-2

16-3

16-4

PICKING STRIKE TWO

When intending to "pick" strike two, be sure to chamber your stick long enough to alert your opponent to the fact that you are preparing to attack him from that angle (Figure 16-5). Allow your stick to move about two-thirds of the distance to its false target (Figure 16-6). As the opponent commits his defense (in this case, a roof block), change the angle of your attack and strike your opponent's unguarded midsection (Figure 16-7).

16-5

16-6

16-7

PICKING STRIKE THREE

When intending to "pick" strike three, be sure to chamber your stick long enough to alert your opponent to the fact that you are preparing to attack him from that angle (Figure 16-8). Allow your stick to move about two-thirds of the distance to its false target (Figure 16-9). As the opponent commits his defense (in this case, a cross block), change the angle of your attack and strike your opponent's temple (Figure 16-10). Immediately follow this with another change of angle (in the event that he is able to block your first feint), and strike his throat (Figure 16-11).

16-8

16-9

16-10

16-11

PICKING AS A TRAINING DRILL

Students are first taught how to properly execute the picks or feinting striking combinations and later how to defend against them as well. It takes a keen sense of timing and coordination to execute these techniques and an even greater reflex control and coordination to defend against an opponent's onslaught of them. There exists no pattern to feinting techniques execution because these "picks" are predicated on being deceptive and unpredictable. The sequence of strikes is largely dictated by an opponent's attacks, defensive movements, and general reactions to your movements.

Reversing

Reversing is the name given to the skills used in counterattacking a counterattack. In other words, if you strike an opponent and he blocks and counters you, your counter of his counter is known as a "reversal." And while you may not literally be "reversing" any actual motion, you are attempting to reverse the outcome of the encounter with this approach.

Angel Cabales "reverses" Kimball Joyce's attack.

In the Cabales serrada system, there is a reversal for every movement in every counter. For example, against the standard inside block and counter for strike one, there is a reversal for the initial block, the horizontal counterstrike, the underhand wrist strike, the check, the overhand wrist strike, and the locking sequence. Thus, conceptually, reversing gives the serrada practitioner the ability to counter an opponent six different times and in six different ways against this very basic counter sequence.

The concept and strategy of reversing is an advanced part this art. And in an even more advanced line, there are methods of reversing every reversal an opponent may know and use against your counter to his counter. This is known as "reverse reversing."

Sticky Stick

"Sticky stick" is an advanced combat strategy in Cabales serrada escrima that uses the opponent's own weapon as a guide to striking his weapon-holding hand. As mentioned earlier, attacking the weapon-holding hand is the most basic and primary method of severely injuring and/or disarming an armed opponent, and thus a fast method of ending a confrontation.

The concept of "sticky stick" works like this: an opponent strikes, you move off his line of attack and block his stick with your stick, and rather than moving your stick away from his to counterstrike him, you maintain a check on his stick with your stick while sliding your stick down the shaft of his to the base, thereby striking his hand. This is an advanced counter method and combat strategy that is difficult to defend against. And since your stick never looses contact with your opponent's, there is no block that can be employed to defend against it. What is available, however, are reversing maneuvers.

CHAPTER 17

MENTAL AND EMOTIONAL CONTROL

At the outset of any physical confrontation, it is imperative that you be acutely aware of your surroundings and your opponent. You must also be aware of and accept the fact that at the onset of a fight your body will go through a physiological change. During the moments prior to the commencement of combat, your mind will be working much the same as it is right now. Immediately after the conflict begins, however, you will be unable to think, or worry, about what or who is behind you or if your opponent is armed. These things must be determined by a "pre-combat" mind. It is because of this that the escrimadors train their visual awareness (through the training drills) to take notice of minute details and train their physical skills on the assumption that they will be defending against multiple opponents at all times. Once you engage an opponent, you will generally become intently focused on the destruction of your foe and inherent reactions will have taken over, dictating your responses. Your visual and auditory awareness will slow down to near stop-frame. Your mind or thought process, depending on how it has been developed, will speed up.

What has been termed "tunnel vision" is a characteristic that the escrimador must learn to accept and keep under control. When involved in a physical confrontation for the first time, many people pick a focal point, and everything outside of that point becomes fuzzy. Although having an unwavering focal point seems like a good idea, it is not. Putting all of your attention on one area (e.g., an attacking arm, chest, head) may increase your chances of successfully defending against or attacking that area, but it will decrease your awareness of your surroundings. Cabales serrada escrima exponents understand that there is a good possibility that they may be forced into confronting multiple opponents, and so develop their peripheral vision through the practice of the lock and block drill.

Often, for those experiencing an actual fight for the first couple of times, their tunnel vision gets so bad that it decreases to a point no bigger than the size of a man's head, and they become unaware of anything happening outside of this focal point. This happens because their minds are not used to, and are hence unable to deal with, the unexpected rush of adrenaline and fear of the situation. The practitioners of serrada escrima look to lessen the apparent threat of the unknowns of combat through realistic sparring with weapons and empty-hand defenses against them. Through these sparring sessions, the escrimador experiences simulated combat that is in many ways more threatening than an actual confrontation.

By training with weapons, and making physical contact with those of your opponent, you will develop emotional intensity and greater spiritual willingness to take on and accept the many challenge of combat and life. These qualities are manifested through escrima training because if you miscalculate a strike and miss a block, you will be struck by your opponent's weapon. You must also have the willpower, bravery, and faith in your techniques to walk into an opponent's furious attack, facing certain injury if your techniques fail.

Emotional control is another attribute that an escrimador must deal with, especially during a physical confrontation. Only when you have control over your emotions will you develop in a proper and efficient manner. Your ability to perform is determined by your degree of self-control when placed in a stressful situation.

Relaxation is a fundamental method of controlling the stress-related feelings that cause anxiety. Anxiety is detrimental to your ability to perform in a given moment. The most important attribute for a martial artist is to be able to perform in the moment. You must have a calm state of mind and be free from tension. If your body is tense, it must first relax before it can initiate a technique, thus lengthening reaction time. Relaxation exercises can assist you in controlling your emotions when you are in an anxious state. Some relaxation exercises include taking long and deep breaths, meditation, listening to soothing music, and various stretching exercises.

As you mature during your pursuit of knowledge and become proficient in escrima, greater self-discipline, self-esteem, and self-confidence will result. The vast physical, emotional, and mental improvements escrima training gives you will enable you to better handle the world's unpredictability.

AFTERWORD

Close examination of the photographs included herein shows variations in posture, movement, and timing among the instructors of the
art, thus indicating that the art continued to evolve during Cabales' life-
time and was not frozen in time as many choose to believe. Moreover,
the only true "secret" to a martial art is obtaining an understanding of
its essence, and not rote duplication of the postures and movements
of a single individual (e.g., the founder or master of an art). When the
essence is understood, one is then able to transcend the art and apply
it as needed and as suits one's body type and personality. For as Angel
Cabales used to say, "Once you have the key, you can open any lock."
The figurative "key" in serrada escrima (and indeed in any martial art)
is its underlying concepts, principles, and strategies.

While Angel Cabales always told his students to keep his art pure, it
can be said that there is truly no "pure" art of Cabales serrada escrima.
Angel Cabales certainly took what was taught him by his teacher and
reworked it to fit his personality and the needs of his America-based
students. And Cabales continued to evolve, to make adjustments to
existing techniques, and to otherwise develop his system until his passing in 1991. As examples: Cabales added a number of the empty-hand
locks to the system, which were said to not have been part of Dizon's
system; Cabales added the kicking techniques, courtesy of his early top
student Dentoy Revillar; Cabales added a systematic ranking structure
and adjusted the curriculum accordingly, courtesy of Mike Inay; and
over the three decades Cabales taught his art, his teaching method
and his technique execution also changed, if only in minor ways. As
a result, students of different generations, although having studied the
same art under the same master, have different views on it and perform
its movements in slightly different ways. Thus, what is thought to be
"pure" to students from one era, is believed to be "incorrect" to students
of another. And yet, it is still the same art.

Cabales serrada escrima, like all other practices, is an art form. It is the knowledge and understanding of a skill. It is reacting and performing under the stress of an emotional or physical confrontation. For hundreds of years, escrimadors have improved their abilities by applying their knowledge about combat, and it is this knowledge that constitutes a science. Thus, Cabales serrada escrima as physically practiced and taught is an *art;* however, the organized knowledge underlying its practice may be referred to as a *science.*

As science evolves, so should art. In Cabales serrada escrima, as in other martial arts, practitioners learn from trial and error. There is no place to turn to for guidance in the midst of combat other than the knowledge and experience that lies within. The scientific approach of Cabales serrada escrima is based on clear concepts, theories, and principles that Grandmaster Angel Cabales developed from experimentation and analysis of the physical movements of the decuerdas style. Thus, it is up to the next generation of Cabales serrada escrima master instructors to keep the evolution process alive without abandoning the established concepts, theories, and principles that form the nucleus of the system. And indeed a number of Angel Cabales' former students, such as Dentoy Revillar, Mike Inay, Jimmy Tacosa, and Rene Latosa, have followed in their master's footsteps, expanding and otherwise developing the knowledge passed on to them to suit their own personality and needs.

When all is said and done, the outer aesthetics of the art are irrelevant. Rather, it is the inner workings—the essence—that has stood the test of time, and is perhaps the only thing that can be considered "pure" in the style. Moreover, as long as one stays true to the core concepts, principles, and strategies, one not only remains "pure" in terms of perpetuating the art, but will discover the key to unlocking not only the offensive and defensive techniques of an opponent, but the infinite applications and permutations of the basic techniques within the Cabales serrada system itself. It can be said, then, that this understanding, and the ability to apply the knowledge, is the only real "secret" to this fighting art or any other.

In closing, I would like to quote Frank Rillamas, one of the masters of the Cabales serrada system, who summed up the feelings of everyone who was fortunate enough to spend time with the late master, when he said: "The twelve years (1979–91) I spent with Angel was and always will be a great honor. Our time together, whether it be to practice, or just to watch him demonstrate his exceptional skills, and even just to be around him was a blessing that I will cherish forever."

. . . And so will we all.

Mabuhay ang Cabales serrada escrima!

Appendix A

LINEAGE OF CABALES SERRADA ESCRIMA

While this is not a definitive lineage of the art, it is offered as a means of promoting those who both received their master's degree from Angel Cabales, and also those who may not have, but who have certainly excelled in the art and done much to perpetuate it. And while there were only sixteen diplomas awarded for the rank of *pangulong guro* (master instructor), there were more than sixty awarded for the rank of *pangalawang guro* (advanced instructor), and many more for *pang-isa guro* (basic instructor). In addition, there are a number of long-time practitioners of the art who studied under Angel Cabales before his ranking structure was initiated, who thus received no rank.

With this in mind, while the following lists are a good indicator of qualified instructors, it must in no way be construed as being complete. And so I offer my apologies to the many other students of Grandmaster Cabales who are not listed here and yet continue to perpetuate his art in an honorable way. Moreover, in keeping with Cabales serrada in particular, and not serrada escrima in general, only direct disciples of Angel Cabales are included here. This is not to say, however, that the second-generation practitioners of the art who have received their instructor credentials under Cabales' students are not qualified to carry on the tradition. They certainly are.

Master Graduates of the Cabales Escrima Academy

Johnny Cabales, Vincent Cabales, Jimmy Tacosa, Jaime "JC" Cabiero, Ron Saturno, Lee Foster, Kimball Joyce (Sultan Uddin), Wade Williams, Frank Rillamas, Gabriel Asuncion, Darren Tibon, Jerry Preciado, Khalid Khan, Mark Wiley, Rey Tap, and Chuck Cadell.

Other Notable Instructors Under Angel Cabales

Dentoy Revillar, Rene Latosa, Mike Inay, Al Concepcion, Art Miraflor, Dan Inosanto, Ted Lucay Lucay (deceased), Carlito Bonjoc, Jr., Anthony Davis, Mike Davis, Joe Gastello, JoJo Soriben, Graciela Casillas, among others.

Appendix B

ORIGINAL OUTLINE FOR BOOK SERIES

This is the original outline of how Grandmaster Angel Cabales wanted to present his art in a series of six books. And while such a series was never published, it is presented here as an appendix for its historical value, because it sheds light on how the late master envisioned the related elements or components of his art.

Volume One: history, stances, footwork, twelve strikes, three single-stick defenses against strikes one through three, and lineage

Volume Two: complete single-stick and stick-and-dagger defensive techniques against strikes one through six

Volume Three: complete single-stick and stick-and-dagger defensive techniques against strikes seven through twelve

Volume Four: complete system of hand-to-hand techniques, including parries, joint locks, body locks/throws

Volume Five: complete system of disarms and reversals with single stick and empty hands

Volume Six: complete system of reflex development, and drills and sparring methods